RHODODENDRONS

WITH
CAMELLIAS and MAGNOLIAS
2001

**THE ROYAL
HORTICULTURAL
SOCIETY**

Published in 2001 by
The Royal Horticultural Society,
80 Vincent Square, London SW1P 2PE

ISBN 1 902896 05 X

Edited for the RHS by Karen Wilson

Honorary Editor for the Rhododendron, Camellia and Magnolia Group
Philip Evans

Editorial Subcommittee
Maurice Foster
Rosemary Foster
Brian Wright

Printed by Page Bros, Norfolk

CONTENTS

COLOURED ILLUSTRATIONS

Front cover: Camellia 'Harold L. Paige'. An entry in Class 22 of the Early Camellia Competition. (Photos Great Britain)
Back cover top: Magnolia × brooklynensis 'KO1'. An entry for the Photographic Competition from Rod Wild. *Middle: Camellia* 'Les Jury'. One of the winning trio in Class 18 for Ann Hooton at the Main Camellia Competition (Photos Great Britain). *Bottom: Rhododendron* 'Mrs G. W. Leak' × 'Rouge'. Second prize in Class 32 at the Main Rhododendron Competition for Exbury Gardens (Photos Great Britain)

Fig. 1: Magnolia 'Leda' (Philippe de Spoelberch)
Fig. 2: Magnolia cylindrica (Philippe de Spoelberch)
Fig. 3: Magnolia 'Bjuv' (Philippe de Spoelberch)
Fig. 4: Rhododendron 'Sierra Beauty' (Dr R A Thornton)
Fig. 5: Rhododendron 'Point Defiance' (Dr R A Thornton)
Fig. 6: Rhododendron 'Pied Piper' (Dr R A Thornton)
Fig. 7: Magnolia liliiflora in South Korea (Edward Boscawen)
Fig. 8: Rhododendron yedoense var. *poukhanense* in South Korea (Edward Boscawen)
Fig. 9: Camellia petal blight (Herb Short)
Fig. 10: Camellia petal blight - sclerotia (Herb Short)
Fig. 11: Camellia petal blight - apothecia (Luther W Baxter Jr, Clemson University, USA)
Fig. 12: Rhododendron pudorosum in SE Tibet (Philip Evans)
Fig. 13: Rhododendron aganniphum on the bank of the Cha La, SE Tibet (Philip Evans)
Fig. 14: The view down the Tsari valley (Philip Evans)
Fig. 15: Yellow *Rhododendron phaeochrysum* aff. in SE Tibet (Philip Evans)
Fig. 16: Camellia 'Loretta Feathers' (John Hilliard)
Fig. 17: Camellia 'Mandalay Queen' (John Hilliard)
Fig. 18: Camellia 'Mouchang' (John Hilliard)
Fig. 19: Pieris forrestii at Sheringham Park (The National Trust)
Fig. 20: Rhododendron 'Brittania' (The National Trust)
Fig. 21: The view from the north tower, Sheringham Park (The National Trust)
Fig. 22: Camellia 'Red Cardinal' (Photos Great Britain)
Fig. 23: Magnolia 'Heaven Scent' in Sunderland Terrace (City of Westminster)
Fig. 24: Magnolia campbellii 'Betty Jessel' (J P Chatelard)
Fig. 25: Rhododendron campanulatum (Photos Great Britain)
Fig. 26: Rhododendron fulvum (Photos Great Britain)
Fig. 27: Rhododendron pachysanthum (Photos Great Britain)
Fig. 28: Camellia 'Margaret Davies' (Photos Great Britain)
Fig. 29: Camellia 'Nuccio's Jewel' (Photos Great Britain)
Fig. 30: Camellia 'Diana's Charm' (Photos Great Britain)
Fig. 31: Rhododendron 'Cinnkeys', winner of the Photographic Competition (J L Rees)
Fig. 32: Second in the Photographic Competition, *Magnolia* 'Mark Jury' (Dr George Hargreaves)
Fig. 33: Third in the Photographic Competition, an azalea seedling (John Wilkes-Jones)

BLACK AND WHITE ILLUSTRATIONS

p.21: map of the botanical tour to South Korea (Edward Boscawen)
p.44: The McLaren Challenge Cup, the Loder Challenge Cup, the Crosfield Challenge Cup and the Alan Hardy Challenge Salver (Brian Wright)
p.46: The route of the 1999 expedition to the Tsari Valley (Philip Evans)

FOREWORD

MAURICE FOSTER

The millennium year provided one of the best spring seasons I can remember for both quantity and quality of flower on all three genera. A previous summer of good growth followed by a mild winter, an absence of spring frost and a plentiful supply of rain at the right time, made the plants sparkle with health and vitality, heavy with flower. As I write now in early September, there is a whiff of autumn in the air and only the great fragrant chalices of *Magnolia grandiflora* remain as a reminder of the abundance of spring. And as you will all know by the time you read this, this autumn marked a change of Chairman. Unfortunately, ill health meant that John Bond had to reduce his many commitments and after three years in the chair he resigned in September.

His resignation was a significant loss to the Group as under his stewardship it prospered and progressed; he brought leadership to the Committee both in resolving residual problems and in creating new opportunities to develop Group activities. John has held senior positions in the RHS for many years and it was not long before he set up closer liaison and cooperation with the Society with tangible benefit to the Group. He was also quick to make organisational and constitutional improvements: notably to entitle all Branch Chairman to attend committee meetings with full voting rights; to create a discretionary category of associate membership for non-RHS members remote from London and to open up committee elections by admitting postal and proxy votes. He also straightened out a number of outstanding anomalies with some of the regional branches.

Instead of simply leaving surplus funds on deposit, John used them to invest in the future by donating themed collections of rhododendrons to established gardens, both to promote the rhododendron and to help raise public awareness of the Group. Two collections were established at Wisley, of rhododendron species and Rustica Flore Pleno hybrids, and a project set up to assemble an historic collection of hardy hybrids at Ramster in Surrey, the home of Mrs Miranda Gunn, our membership secretary. A record of these valuable initiatives appears in this issue of the Year Book (see p.52).

John's was a notably active and enterprising chairmanship. He has brought the Group into a new millennium in confident trim and I know all members will wish to join me in thanking him for his exceptional contribution to its activities; and above all to wish him an early restoration to health.

The Year Book remains the principal focus of interest to many of our members and is central to the success of the Group as a whole. This issue continues the high standards of content and production consistently set by Philip Evans as Editor, with a high level of interest in a broad and balanced range of contributions.

Two short articles – very much to the point – echo the concerns expressed by John Bond in the last issue regarding the fall in popularity of the rhododendron. Peter Cox and Brian Wright each trace reasons for the decline from two quite different perspectives. This is a serious matter and I would like to invite members to put forward their own ideas about the problem by writing to Eileen Wheeler, Editor of the Bulletin. Airing a broad selection of views in the newsletter could stimulate a positive discussion within the Group about what we could and perhaps should be doing to reverse the trend. It could certainly help in finding ways of raising awareness of all that rhododendrons have to offer to the general gardening public, in particular to those 280,000 gardeners represented by the current RHS membership.

Having said that, we should not forget our two other 'subsidiary' genera, *Camellia* and *Magnolia*, which by contrast do not appear to be suffering the same decline in interest. Camellias seem to retain their popularity rather well, notwithstanding petal blight, and magnolias feature more favourably in a discriminating public perception than ever before. In both cases, a widening diversity of plants seems to be opening up a wider range of planting opportunities, and the perception of many gardeners is that camellias and magnolias are not that difficult to grow well and are reasonably trouble free. Which leads me to wish you all unqualified success in growing healthy and forgiving rhododendrons of surpassing excellence in what I'm sure will be the best spring ever, that of 2001.

EDITORIAL

PHILIP EVANS

A quarter of a century ago the late Neil Treseder wrote a short article for the 1975 Year Book about *Magnolia cylindrica*, a species first described from eastern China by E H Wilson in 1927. Treseder explained the reservations he had formed about the authenticity of the plants then distributed in the UK as *M. cylindrica*. These had originated around 1950 as Hilliers' grafts, from plants grown in the USA using seed acquired from China in 1936. In this issue, Philippe de Spoelberch brings the subject of *M. cylindrica* right up to date, by considering some recent seed introductions of the true species and describing the named hybrids and their histories.

Camellia flower blight is a plant disease not as yet fully understood by many camellia growers in the UK. Herb Short has taken time away from his responsibilities as Editor of the *International Camellia Journal* to contribute an article on this subject that imparts both scientific information and practical advice. He is anxious that the information should reach as wide an audience as possible and would be interested to receive from our membership any accounts of experience with the disease. Contact Herb Short, 41 Galveston Road, London SW15 2RZ

Unless one lives in north Norfolk, a visit to Sheringham Park requires a long journey. But a walk around this wonderful local amenity, even if not in the rhododendron flowering season, is an intriguing experience, not least for the occasional mature species (such as *R. calophytum*) rearing up through the vast cover of rhododendron hybrids and (sadly) *R. ponticum*. Keith Zealand, the Head Warden for the National Trust at Sheringham Park, tells us what has been going on there since the National Trust took over, and summarises the present state and prospects of the rhododendron collection originally established by the Upcher family.

Armchair plant hunters will not be disappointed by this edition. They may travel in comfort and safety with Dr Thornton to the west coast of the USA, in his intriguing story of the Southampton connection with the Lem and Lofthouse rhododendron hybrids; or fly east with the Boscawens to the botanical riches of S Korea; or stopover in the Himalayas to look for rhododendrons in Tibet's Tsari valley.

There is, besides, much more of interest and quality contributed to this issue, touching aspects of all three genera.

THE LOST RHODODENDRONS OF SOUTHAMPTON

RAY THORNTON

This is a tale of a grand English garden, an English hybridiser and a Norwegian adventurer, together with a small contribution from a distinguished German family, not normally associated with rhododendrons. Its early beginnings involve Sir Joseph Hooker and a great Cornish garden – Tremough.

The search begins

My involvement in this particular story begins in 1981 when, while working as a biochemist in a company in Southampton, I was sent to Geneva for a two-week management school. In my spare time I visited the Geneva Botanic Garden and found some interesting rhododendrons. On my return, when discussing the visit, and my interest in the genus *Rhododendron*, with my secretary, Mrs Lesli Piper, she enquired if rhododendrons with names related to her family existed. We identified 'Robin Redbreast', for her husband Robin, and 'Pied Piper' (see Fig.6) as appropriate. The former was commercially available in England but the latter was clearly going to be more difficult to obtain. It had just been registered by a Mr J G Lofthouse of Vancouver, Canada, from a cross made by a

man named Halfdan Lem and raised by Mr Arnold Piper (hence the name) and was not available in the UK.

We wrote to Mr Lofthouse and he confirmed the existence of 'Pied Piper' in his garden in Vancouver. Fortunately, at that time I had changed jobs and was now screening scientific literature. I persuaded my employer that it was important to meet the authors of papers personally to get a fuller idea of their work. This would later give me the opportunity to fly to Vancouver, primarily to meet a statistician at the Simon Fraser University, Vancouver, but also to meet Jack Lofthouse.

Leaving Southampton

At about the same time I had met an American who had, in his UK garden, a large collection of rhododendrons bred in the United States, as well as many other hybrids. These included a set of vigorous red cultivars such as 'Etta Burrows', 'Ruby Bowman', 'Markeeta's Flame' and 'Halfdan Lem'. I was most impressed and, judging by the plant named after him, it appeared that Halfdan Lem, whoever he was, had a golden touch at hybridising.

I was also at this time expanding my

knowledge of rhododendrons by buying old Year Books. The 1948 Year Book came my way with an article on hybridising by Fred Rose VMH, formerly of Townhill Park, Swaythling, Southampton, once the home of Lord Swaythling. (This garden had already introduced such rhododendrons as 'David' FCC and 'Gladys Rose' AM.) Mr Rose referred to carefully-thought-out crosses made in 1939 from which he expected good results:

> Then came the second World War and we were compelled to abandon practically all work on Rhododendrons, Lilies and other ornamental plants and concentrate on food production. We did, however, sow the 1939 seeds, and the plants were put into nursery beds. They received no further attention, became overcrowded and suffered from drought. As a result we lost many of the crosses.

At the end of the war Townhill Park was sold. But Rose goes on to say, 'It is interesting to record that I sent seed of most of the 1939 crosses to a correspondent in Seattle, Washington. He was successful with them and it is pleasing to know many of those hybrids are now popular in America.'

I checked the list of Group members in the 1939 Year Book for the unknown correspondent and found that, in addition to most of the royal families of Europe, there were two possible correspondents in the Seattle area, Halfdan Lem, Seattle, and Mrs H L Larson, North Tacoma, Washington State. It was interesting to note that both Lem and Larson (Hjalmar) had Norwegian names. Many Norwegians had emigrated to the Pacific North West in the United States.

But Halfdan Lem seemed the most obvious choice, and I wrote to Lord Swaythling, then living in the Channel Islands; he confirmed Lem was the correspondent.

The parents

Inspection of the recorded parentage of Lem's hybrids suggested that at least two rhododendrons he grew originated from Rose's crosses in Southampton. These were 'Anna' and 'Red Loderi'. The former is a cross of 'Norman Gill' × 'Jean Marie de Montague', the second a cross of 'Loderi King George' × 'Earl of Athlone'. 'Anna' (registered in 1952) was used by Lem in many of his subsequent crosses, and appears to have been one of his favourites.

The ancestry of 'Anna' (⅝ *R. griffithianum*, ⅛ *R. arboreum*, ¼ unknown) is interesting. 'Norman Gill', the first parent, is a cross of 'Beauty of Tremough' with *R. griffithianum* and was registered by the Cornish nursery firm of Richard Gill, based at Tremough on land leased from the Shilson family. 'Beauty of Tremough' is itself a hybrid of *R. arboreum* crossed with *R. griffithianum*.

Richard Gill's *R. griffithianum*, used in these crosses, has a fascinating history which was discussed by Lionel de Rothschild in *The Rhododendron Story* (1996). Quoting his grandfather Lionel, he said that the form of *R. griffithianum* used by a 20th century hybridizer, Lowinsky, had come from Gill, was known as 'roseum superbum' and produced very tender offspring. Millais, in his 1917 book *Rhododendrons and the various hybrids,* states that Henry Shilson of Tremough was a great friend of Sir Joseph Hooker and that the great botanist sent his friend large numbers of seeds from the first collection made in Sikkim. As *R. griffithianum* was discovered at this time by Hooker (and named for a curator of the Calcutta Botanic Garden), a plausible link back to the 1850s from 'Anna's *R. griffithianum* parentage can be inferred.

'Jean Marie de Montague', 'Anna's second parent, is itself a cross of *R. griffithianum* with an unknown hybrid. It is not therefore surprising that 'Anna' and its descendents have spectacular flowers; the hardiness is somewhat better than would have been predicted and presumably red is dominant to white in the hybrids. 'Red Loderi' is something of a mystery, apparently not registered, but I have seen a plant with this name growing in New Zealand. Again there is quite a lot of *R. griffithianum* in the hybrid.

It is interesting to note that this theme of hybridising was soon picked up elsewhere in the US. Thus the impressive 'Markeeta's Flame', that I came across in my American friend's garden, is a cross of 'Anna' with 'Loderi Venus'.

Lem and Lofthouse hybrids

By the time I took my business trip to Vancouver, and visited Jack Lofthouse, I therefore had a pretty good idea of the origin of many of Lem's hybrids and indeed the later hybrids from Jack Lofthouse. After I had

concluded my business at Simon Fraser University in Vancouver (surely one of the most attractive university campuses in the world), I travelled out to meet Jack Lofthouse in north Vancouver. I was in for a surprise. He has quite a small garden and most of his early hybrids, and plants hybridized by Lem, occupy the ground in his garden. They are by no means small plants. The rest live in pots around his plot, or 'yard' in North American terminology. Of necessity therefore Darwin's theories of natural selection are pursued with a vengeance here. Only a few seedlings, those meeting Jack Lofthouse's critical inspection when very small plants, survive, but plenty of registered plants have been produced nevertheless. On a subsequent visit to Vancouver I was shown many Lofthouse hybrids growing in the garden at the rival, older university, the University of British Columbia (UBC), which also has excellent magnolias luxuriating in the rather wet Pacific North West climate. There is also an excellent collection of Lofthouse hybrids at Cross Hills Garden, Kimbolton, New Zealand.

Jack Lofthouse confirmed the story of Halfdan Lem, whom he knew, and Mrs Lofthouse hinted that Lem was somewhat larger than life, as are many of his hybrids. Flamboyant might be the right word. Needless to say, later that year a number of scions arrived at my house in Southampton, with a phytosanitary certificate. Despite a postal delay, a surprisingly large number rooted under bottom heat in somewhat primitive apparatus: no mist but a polythene sheet to maintain humidity. Scions were treated for 24 hours with a dilute solution of Indole-3-butyric acid, as described by David Leach in *Rhododendrons of the World*. The scions included 'Lem's Cameo' which is said to be difficult to root. The rest were a good mixture of Lem and Lofthouse hybrids.

Return to Southampton

So, a wide variety of Lem and derived Lofthouse hybrids had returned to Southampton nearly 50 years after their parents had left. Many are now well known in commerce and some are available in the UK. Of the Lem introductions 'Anna', 'Lem's Cameo', 'Lem's Storm Cloud', 'Point Defiance' (see Fig. 5) and 'Pied Piper' are all excellent. 'Lem's Pink Walloper' is also good if your taste is for bold plants. 'Anna' is occasionally available and I have seen it at the Wisley Plant Centre. The bold 'Halfdan Lem' seems to be reasonably widely available.

Of the Lofthouse crosses, many of which derive from Lem's plants, those in the Lem tradition of large bold plants include 'Sierra Beauty' (see Fig. 4) and 'Sierra Sunrise'. In my garden these are very fast growing with spectacularly large trusses in mid-May. Their growth rate is only exceeded by some related hybrids, described later. Other large Lofthouse hybrids include 'Lady of Spain', a nice crimson, and the aptly named 'Cherry Float'. Jack Lofthouse used an ever widening range of plants for his later crosses. As some are not well known in the UK, I mention 'Sierra del Oro' ('Crest' × *R. lacteum*) and 'Oh! Canada', a striking yellow-orange, similar to 'Jalisco Janet' with a maple-leaf shaped coloration in the throat

(apparently not registered). This is one of my favourites. I also have 'Butter Brickle' from the same cross as 'Nancy Evans', but perhaps not quite as good. 'Yellow Petticoats' is close to 'Hotei'. 'Party Package' is a pretty frilly pink, with new foliage similar to a camellia. Other Lofthouse crosses included a number of *R. yakushimanum* crosses, more to my taste than some of this race; 'Canadian Sunset' (pink, fading) and 'Snowstorm' (white) are two of my favourites.

In later years Lofthouse produced a number of 'doubles' with a large calyx. I had 'Sunup-Sundown', but it marked badly when it rained. 'Pink Porcelain' is better, but still suffers from this habit to some extent. A still later series of Lofthouse crosses such as 'Silver Trumpets' have developed the double theme more successfully, but I do not have this particular plant.

Jack Lofthouse and his wife Edie visited England in the late 1980s. As they were visiting Exbury Gardens, two miles away from my home, they called and inspected my efforts at growing North American rhododendrons. 'Fred Wyniatt' was flowering at that time and Jack immediately suggested crossing it with one of his, 'Cherry Custard', to improve it. This I did, producing a number of quite nice yellow-pink hybrids. The best of these I plan to register under the name 'Challenger' after one of the Short C-class flying boats which were based in Southampton Water just prior to the Second World War. Another cross I have made is of 'Canadian Beauty' (a Lofthouse cross close to the 'Wallopers' of Lem) also with 'Fred Wyniatt'. This produced about seven mammoth seedlings. The best I have tentatively named 'Corinna', after another of the flying boats.

I thought that these seedlings might be world record holders for rapid growth but this title may pass to 'Lem's Pink Walloper' × *R. diaprepes* 'Gargantua', from the RHS Seed Exchange service, which is growing at an extraordinary rate especially after this wet spring. I also have some nice crosses from 'Lem's Cameo' for which I have some hopes.

Perhaps I should mention that Hjalmar Larson, Lem's fellow Norwegian, also produced some fine plants. I have 'Etta Burrows', a *R. strigillosum* cross, and very near to that species, and 'Bergie Larson', presumably the Mrs H L Larson referred to in the 1939 Year Book.

Seeds derived from Larson crosses are available and I have some plants of 'Robert Louis Stevenson' crossed with 'Orange Marmalade', which are dwarf with a wide range of colours from orange through red.

I should add that when *The Rhododendron Story* arrived in 1996, I was pleased to find confirmation and additional information in the article by Pat Halligan on American hybridizers. I should also mention that Jack Lofthouse recently received the Silver Medal of the American Rhododendron Society in recognition of his many hybrids.

Had the Second World War not taken place, more of Fred Rose's crosses would no doubt have been developed in Southampton, but at least Halfdan Lem knew when he was on to a good thing. Thanks to his efforts and a stroke of good fortune that led me to both the Lem and Lofthouse hybrids, Fred Rose's carefully planned crosses and their descendants – with a lineage going back to the discovery of *R. griffithianum* in the Sikkim-Himalayas by Sir Joseph Hooker and the early hybridizing of Richard Gill – live on.

References

POSTAN, CYNTHIA, (1996). *The Rhododendron Story*. Royal Horticultural Society, London.

MILLAIS, J. G. (1917). *Rhododendrons and the various hybrids*. Longmans, Green & Co., London.

LEACH, DAVID (1962). *Rhododendrons of the World*. Allen & Unwin, London.

Dr Ray Thornton is a member of the Group and lives and gardens near Southampton where he has an extensive collection of rhododendrons and magnolias

RHODODENDRON SPECIES STUDY WEEKEND, EDINBURGH

ROBBIE JACK

Following an immediate and positive response to his suggestion in the December 1999 Bulletin, Dr Robbie Jack organised the study session on the identification of rhododendron species for April 2000. It took the form of a study weekend at the Royal Botanic Garden Edinburgh under the tutorship of Dr David Chamberlain. His willingness to run the course and the superb facilities there determined the venue. The event comprised a very successful and stimulating series of study sessions which were attended by 22 members of the Group.

Building on basic botanical knowledge, laboratory microscopes were used to familiarize the group with the diagnostic features of scales, hairs, leaves and flowers while the framework of rhododendron classification and botanical keys were discussed. The laboratory sessions were then alternated with sessions in the garden which provided an ideal opportunity to combine both careful detailed scrutiny in the working laboratory with actual growing plants. In particular it helped to consolidate the recognition of those features used to distinguish closely related species by seeing them growing in proximity to each other. This brought together a wealth of species which even in the wild would have been impossibly scattered, in some cases hundreds of miles apart. This wonderful living reference collection of rhododendrons held by RBG Edinburgh was ideal for the Group's study and enjoyment. We saw more than 150 species in flower over that weekend with only a few showing frost damage.

A further session lead by Dr George Argent involved a demonstration of electron microscopy and its use in the analysis and classification of Vireya rhododendrons. This was followed by an inspection of the huge collection of wild-sourced Vireyas, many in flower in the controlled environment glasshouse section. As it was from these plants that the 1998 RHS London Flower Show Gold Medal exhibit was drawn, we were in effect treated to a hugely expanded version of that display.

There was so much to see that it was after 6pm before we left the garden for the day. But the day was not over, for the evening afforded an opportunity to entertain Dr Chamberlain, Dr Argent and their wives to dinner. A very lively and enjoyable evening was rounded off with an excellent slide show of plant collecting in the wild by Dr Chamberlain from his own expeditions – a memorable day indeed.

The study progressed on the second

day to the herbarium, which gave an insight into the professional taxonomist's use of herbarium specimens and comparison of similar material from different geographical sources. This in turn was related to the comprehensive range of scientific library texts and live wild-origin material in the garden, and was finally exemplified in our own working handbooks. We were further shown how techniques like chemical finger-printing of leaf waxes is helping to solve inter-species and even inter-sectional relationships. The overall picture was of the dynamic state of rhododendron taxonomy. Our members did indeed virtually look over the taxonomist's shoulder and see both technical problems as well as solutions.

Lunch that day was at Glendoick Gardens near Perth where Peter Cox and his wife Patricia led the party round part of their superb garden. Again the emphasis was on taxonomy. It was especially interesting to view plants from wild-collected seed, and consider their species

affinities and their source locations at the same time. Among many uncommon species there were new recent discoveries, some yet to flower for the first time – another dynamic aspect of the genus *Rhododendron.*

This hard working, interest packed, hands on, stimulating weekend was enthusiastically enjoyed by all. Above all the unflagging keenness of the participants was noted and appreciated by the Group's hosts and tutors.

Acknowledgements
The Group was greatly indebted to the RBG Edinburgh for the laboratory facilities, materials and staff and to Mr and Mrs Cox at Glendoick Gardens.

Dr Robbie Jack is a member of the Executive Committee of the Group. He is also a member of the RHS Rhododendron and Camellia Committee. He lives near Lanark in Scotland

MAGNOLIA CYLINDRICA

PHILIPPE DE SPOELBERCH

Recent introductions from China seem to indicate that true *Magnolia cylindrica* is a much more discrete plant than that which has been grown in our gardens under this name for the last 50 years. As it is found in Anhui Province of China, and in particular on the Huang Shan, *M. cylindrica* presents a small flower with six narrow tepals sub-tended by three sepaloid tepals which fall before the flowers fades, whereas the well known hybrid (now named 'Pegasus') shows nine petaloid tepals of a strong texture and which flower profusely.

The true *M. cylindrica* (see Fig. 2) can be identified, even when not in flower, by the following characteristics:
* branchlets silvery pubescent
* leaves elliptic, nearly oblanceolate
* lower surface of the leaves pulverulent to glaucous and quite visible from a distance

(A full description can be found on pages 115-18 of *Magnolia and their Allies.*[1])

The plant starts life as an upright growing tree and clearly would continue to do so if given sufficient warmth during the summer months.

Because of the presence of sepaloid tepals, *M. cylindrica* could be confused with *M. kobus*, but the upright candle-like poise of the flower and spatulate tepals might help in identifying the species.

The recent introductions from China initiated by Charles Tubesing of The Magnolia Society provided for a fresh look at this taxon. Seed from South Anhui Province (Holden Arboretum 87-86, from 31°N, 117°E) was grown at the Holden Arboretum and seedlings were distributed to magnolia growers around the world. The first plants to flower and form fruits at the Holden have clearly demonstrated the particular status of the taxon. It had previously been placed in section Buergeria on account of its sepaloid tepals. But in his recent revision (*Magnoliaceae Hardy in Cooler Temperate Regions*[2]), Spongberg has found it useful to create a new section on its own for this special plant. The behaviour of the fruit is the cause of this taxonomic change. It is quite curious that no one ever noticed the early decomposition of the fruit, which occurs well before the seed are dropped: 'follicles dehiscing … falling away individually or in irregular masses'.

A tree similar to the Holden introduction is growing in Roy Lancaster's garden, in Hampshire. The 'Shanghai form', as David Hunt has called it, is particularly dainty with a narrow waist showing half way between the base and the expanding tip of the tepals. Another introduction

g. 1: Magnolia *'Leda'* (M. cylindrica ×
campbellii *var.* alba?) *see p.18*

Fig. 2: The true Magnolia cylindrica *(Holden '87/86)
see p.16*

g. 3: Magnolia *'Bjuv', a hybrid of* M. cylindrica *(see p.17)*

Fig. 4 (above): Rhododendron *'Sierra Beauty'*, a *Lofthouse hybrid (see p.12). Fig. 5 (below left):* R. *'Point Defiance'*, a Lem hybrid *(see p.12). Fig. 6 (below right):* R. *'Pied Piper'*, another Lem hybrid *(see p.9)*

Fig. 7 (right): Magnolia liliiflora *at Ch'omsongdae, South Korea (see p.23).*
Fig. 8 (below): Rhododendron yedoense *var.* poukhanense *in a Temple Garden, Seoul, South Korea (see p.20)*

CAMELLIA PETAL BLIGHT

Fig. 9: Camellia Petal Blight. The calyx has been removed to show the ring of white at the base of the flower. Brown patches at the base harden to become sclerotia (see p.31)

Fig. 10: Sclerotia - note on some the shape of the flower base, and one has retained the white ring

Fig. 11: Apothecia - tan, saucer-shaped mushrooms that grow from the sclerotia on the surface of the soil

from China via Karl E Flinck and the Arnold Arboretum (where the mother plant grows) is *Magnolia cylindrica* 'Bjuv' (see Fig. 3). This form grows a very short compact flower, darkly deep purple at the base. All three varieties can be seen in illustrations 90 to 98 of *Magnolia and their Allies*. *M. cylindrica* 'Bjuv' is surely of garden value, a striking note of purple in an otherwise perfectly white section Buergeria collection in the first days of spring – particularly for those northern gardens unable to grow the great Yulania species. Karl Flinck has argued with me that 'Bjuv' could be a cross of *M. cylindrica* with *M. liliiflora*. Other than the purple colouring, it has nothing in common with that taxon, and it flowers much too early. Many self-pollinated seedlings growing here at Herkenrode[3] may provide a clue as to the parentage of this cultivar.

It is often said that there are two forms of *M. cylindrica:* one upright, the other a low growing, compact shrub. I think that this has all to do with climate and lack of summer heat. The great *M. cylindrica* at the Henry Foundation (now determined to be a hybrid) shows the strength of this tree if it is given a good baking in summer.

It is a pity that Johnstone had not seen *M. cylindrica* when he published his *Asiatic Magnolia in Cultivation*[4]. Previous seed introductions to England, by Wilson, had not germinated and Johnstone could only comment that 'scions attributed to this species have lately been imported from America so that grafted plants should be available to us before long'. With his keen eye for observation of details, he would have noticed the peculiar dehiscing

conditions of this taxon. The scions probably originated from the collection at The Henry Foundation in Gladwyne, Pennsylvania. The big *M. cylindrica* tree at the Foundation has recently shown signs of decay. Cut back to a stump, it still managed to produce a crop of flowers proving that this original Lu Shan introduction was a hybrid (Dick Figlar personal communication). We shall never know where the happy cross occurred.

Both *M. cylindrica* and *M. denudata* grow together in nature as has been described by Richard Pearson, and this would explain the two introductions:

On May 5 and 6 1984, I was fortunate enough to hike through the Huang Shan mountains of Anhui Province, south of the Yangtze river in China. These mountains are an isolated group of jagged scenic peaks, the highest of which are over 1800m. Their location is 30°1 North, 118°1 East. They are famous for their cloudy, misty scenery and luxuriant vegetation. The average temperature being 17.7 °C in July and August, and –3°C in January. In the area surrounding the Beihai Pavilion, reached by a half-day hike up thousands of stone steps leading from the bus terminus, *Magnolia denudata* and *Magnolia cylindrica* could be seen in full flower.

The fact is that the hybrid *M. cylindrica* is the better of the two plants. It is much hardier than *M. denudata* and more spectacular than *M. cylindrica*. One may suppose that the Lushan Botanical Garden having identified the better plant, collected seed on the hybrid for inclusion on their *Index Seminum*. This is probably what they shipped to Mrs J Norman Henry who seems the source of plants grown in the Western world since 1936.

Obviously it would be interesting to cross *M. cylindrica* with *M. denudata* to see if the much-appreciated hybrids can be produced by controlled pollination.

Magnolia cylindrica hybrids

The most widely available of the hybrids is the densely and profusely flowering 'Pegasus', long sold by Hillier's as *M. cylindrica* and rightly much appreciated in all gardens for its spectacular flowering. As it ages, the shrub (in maritime climates) or tree (in warm continental environment) will develop a mass of short, secondary branchlets, like an old pear tree. Several flower buds will develop in a network of crisscrossing buds and branchlets. Flowers are so numerous that they become entangled. It is impossible to count the individual flowers.

It will be important to establish the true 'Pegasus' in our collections. Of the 14 magnolias that entered the collection at Herkenrode under a *M. cylindrica* label, at least four can be described as good candidates for a 'Pegasus' label. They came from good houses such as Hillier, Eisenhut, Spinners and Esveld. Yet I do not know if I have the true 'Pegasus'. This taxon is at Chyverton and was illustrated by Margaret Stones and used for the cover of *Magnolia and their Allies*. The editor and myself were most uncomfortable with the taxonomy of

that beautiful plant and this gave rise, after consultation with Roy Lancaster, to the selected cultivar name 'Pegasus' for what was considered to be a hybrid. Molecular research to be conducted at the University of Reading on behalf of The Magnolia Society may determine if *M. denudata* is indeed the other parent.

'Pegasus' is probably the parent of a couple of spectacular hybrids. I do not think that the true *M. cylindrica* could produce such huge flowers. We must suspect that 'Pegasus' was at the base of these chance crosses:

'Albatross' ('Pegasus' × *M veitchii* 'P. Veitch') of Lanhydrock has the typical cup-and-saucer shaped flower inherited from *M. campbellii* and indeed some growers consider that this might be the real parent not *M.* 'Peter Veitch'. It is reputed to be cold hardy down to zone 6.

'Leda' ('Pegasus' × *M. campbellii* 'Alba'?), with nine tepals, cup-and-saucer, creamy white flowers of thick texture, was raised at Bulk nursery (Boskoop, Netherlands) where the original plant still grows. Grafts of this plant were distributed by Esveld, for many years, under the name *M. cylindrica*; it provided good surprises for his customers. The pollen parent is totally putative, but the flower buds, the habit of the tree and the cup-and-saucer characteristic link it surely with *M. campbellii*. It is a vigorous upright growing hardy plant. The three inner tepals remain folded upright in a twisted and pointed conical poise, whereas the six outer tepals reflex in a quite unique way (see Fig. 1).

Magnolia cylindrica is difficult to grow from cuttings. Scions from very young plants may be easier to root; older plants soon lose this ability. One really has to take cuttings from cuttings. The hybrids with *M. campbellii* 'Alba' have to be grafted.

References

[1] SPONGBERG, DR STEPHEN A (1998) '*Magnoliaceae* hardy in cooler temperate regions' from *Magnolias and their Allies,* published for the International Dendrology Society and The Magnolia Society, being the Proceedings of an International Symposium at Royal Holloway University of London, 1996.

[2] See Note 1

[3] Herkenrode. The author's garden and collection at Wespelar, Belgium.

[4] JOHNSTONE, G H (1955). *Asiatic Magnolias in Cultivation.*

Vicomte Philippe de Spoelberch is a Belgian member of the Group. He is President of the Belgian Dendrology Society, a Council Member of the International Dendrology Society and a Board Member of The Magnolia Society

A Botanical Tour in South Korea

Anne Boscawen

15 April

We were greeted in Seoul by Mr Min Pyong-gal (Carl Ferris Miller), our kind host, and introduced to Mr Song Kihun, Head of the Plant Collections Department, Chollipo Arboretum, who was to be our very knowledgeable botanical guide.

We then boarded our bus, for a tour of some of the more interesting dendrological sites in Seoul. In the grounds at the Kyonbok Palace, we saw *Ulmus parvifolia, Cornus walteri, Diospyros kaki, Pyrus ussuriensis,* with exceptionally large white flowers, *Pinus koraiensis, Cornus controversa, Catalpa ovata* and two very beautiful cherries.

We next stopped to pay homage to a truly amazing two-stemmed lacebark pine, *Pinus bungeana* (introduced many centuries ago), in a garden of terraces formed by large boulders, with drifts of the lavender-mauve *Rhododendron yedoense* and *R. yedoense* var. *poukhanense,* the Korean azalea [1] (see Fig. 8).

The restrained planting of shades of mauve among the grey rocks, with pink *Malus* and magnolia hybrids proved to be very effective.

16 April

We next flew to sub-tropical Cheju Island, and saw grapefruit rolling off the trees as we left the airport. *Daphniphyllum macropodum,* oleanders and *Castanopsis cuspidata* lined the roadway. Later we drove through agricultural country. The land is fertile volcanic soil, but exceedingly stony. The last volcanic eruption was in the 17th century.

Continuing on up towards Halla-san (at 1,950m/6,400ft the highest peak in South Korea) we came to the entrance to the Andok river gorge. The river tumbled down below sheer cliffs, among large grey boulders, and the rocks were festooned with *Hedera rhombea, Piper kadzura* in fruit, *Trachelospermum asiaticum, Ficus nipponica, Kadsura japonica* and the silver trails of *Elaeagnus macrophylla.* The trees clothing the sides of the gorge included *Quercus acuta, Orixa japonica, Cinnamomum japonicum, Euscaphis japonica, Styrax japonica* and *Distylum racemosum.* We saw Korean azaleas, *Arisaema ringens, Calanthe striata* and *C. discolor,* with natural hybrids between the two. There were more wonders round every bend of the river. We were treading on fallen flowers of *Camellia*

---

[1] Rhododendron yedoense *refers to the double, cultivated form, not known in the wild.* Rhododendron yedoense *var.* poukhanense *to the single-flowered wild form, which I will refer to as Korean azalea.*

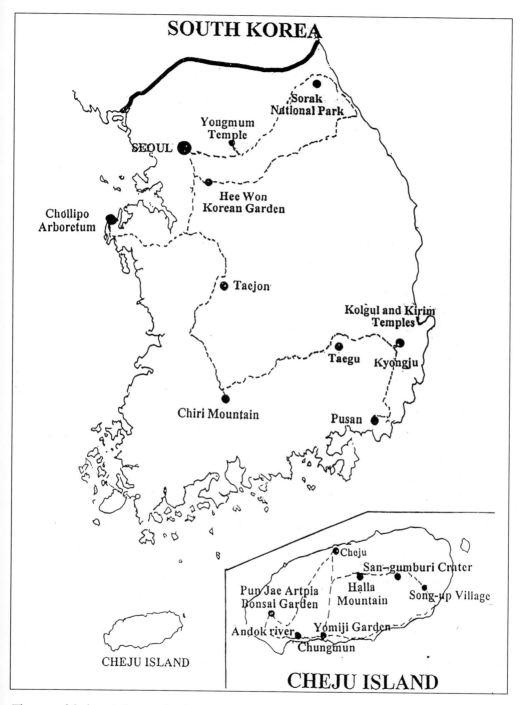

SOUTH KOREA

Sorak
National Park

Yongmum
Temple

SEOUL

Hee Won
Korean Garden

Chóllipo
Arboretum

Taejon

Kolgul and Kirim
Temples

Taegu   Kyongju

Chiri Mountain

Pusan

CHEJU ISLAND

Cheju

San-gumburi Crater

Pun Jae Artpia
Bonsai Garden

Halla
Mountain

Song-up Village

Andok river

Yomiji Garden

Chungmun

CHEJU ISLAND

The route of the botanical tour to South Korea and Cheju Island japonica, and high on the cliffs we could see a coral-coloured bush of the endemic *Rhododendron weyrichii*, with *Fraxinus sieboldiana* in flower beside it. We found *Meliosma myriantha*, *Actinodaphne lancifolia*, *Daphniphyllum macropodum*, *Cleyera japonica*, *Viburnum odoratissimum* and *Pittosporum tobira*. There were few flowers, but this hardly mattered, as the varied foliage looked so wonderful with the waterfalls, the grey cliffs and the stony river.

17 April

We slept at Chungmun, a seaside resort, and then visited the Yomiji Garden which is now 15 years old. It covers 4ha (10 acres) and is the largest indoor Botanic Garden in Asia. There is a large circular conservatory divided into many sections, including Tropical Jungle, Waterlily, Cactus and Tropical Fruit. We travelled through the rest of the grounds in a toy train, to save time, stopping only for the Korean azalea. We presented Mr Kim Mong Chung, the Curator, with *Michelia crassipes*, *Michelia compressa* and *Magnolia coco* as a thank you.

Continuing inland towards Halla Mountain, the natural vegetation changes. In the woods we saw *Daphniphyllum macropodum*, *Cornus controversa*, *C. macrophylla*, *Meliosma myriantha*, *Quercus serrata*, *Q. mongolica*, *Q. aliena*, *Q. variabilis*, *Prunus yedoensis*, *P. leveilleana* Koehne, *P. serrulata*, *Malus sieboldii*, *Abies koreana*, *Photinia villosa* and a deciduous holly, *Ilex macropoda*. Shrubby plants included *Ilex crenata*, *Rhododendron weyrichii*, *Viburnum dilatatum*, *V. furcatum* and *Sasa*

quelpaertensis Nakai – very similar to *S. veitchii* and every bit as rampant. We also saw *Hydrangea petiolaris*, *H.serrata*, and *Schizophragma hydrangeoides*.

Driving on down the mountain, we stopped for an especially lovely view of a wooded valley. All the fresh green deciduous foliage, with the silvery young growth on the evergreen oaks, and here and there a blossoming cherry, made an arresting picture.

Our next stop was for a volcanic crater, San-gumburi, 400m (1,400ft) wide, and 100m (330ft) deep. Sheltered from the wind by the walls of the crater, 420 species of plants grow in this special microclimate. Looking down from the rim, at 308m (1,010ft) altitude, we could see that the broad-leaved trees grew mainly on the south facing side, and the evergreens facing north. At our feet, on the crater's edge, we saw flowers of *Iris uniflora* and *Pulsatilla cernua*. Here too were Korean azalea, and *Stauntonia hexaphylla* in flower, twining through the other shrubs, and deliciously scented.

As we left Cheju Island, we all agreed with Mr Min that we would have needed a whole week to see it properly.

18 April

We drove on to Kyongju City, the early historical capital of Korea. The site has been inhabited for at least 2000 years, and today has a population of 130,000.

In the centre of the city is the Tumuli Park, containing 20 mound tombs of the Shilla Kings, who ruled in the 7th century. Nearby is Ch'omsongdae, a stone tower housing one of the oldest Astronomical

Observatories in East Asia. We discussed the merits of four lovely upright forms of *Magnolia liliiflora* (see Fig. 7) and walked a little further on to the Kyerim Woods where there were many large and grotesquely shaped trees. Most had probably been trimmed for fodder and firewood since ancient times and some were hollow but still living. They included *Celtis sinensis, Zelkova serrata* and *Salix glandulosa* Seemann, an unusually long-lived willow.

19 April

The next day brought bright sunshine and we stopped along the mountain road to look at a view of the mixed deciduous forest. In early spring this is mainly delicate shades of green, from the light pale shades of *Populus simonii* to the mid green of *Zelkova serrata,* and the silvery young foliage of the oaks. *Pinus koraiensis* showed dark along the ridge, and here and there were patches of purple Korean azalea, and pale pink and white cherry blossom.

Our next stop, Kirim-sa, was for a 1300-year-old temple. Walking up through light woodland, we passed tall specimens of *Lindera obtusiloba, L. erythrocarpa* and *L. glauca,* also *Meliosma myriantha, Styrax shiraiana, Carpinus tcshonoskii, Diospyros lotus* and *Cornus controversa* with *Weigela subsessilis* in flower. There were also many *Acer pseudosieboldianum* (Pax) Komarov.

The temple was decorated with thousands of coloured lanterns and streamers, to celebrate the birthday of Buddha. By the entrance was a big *Abies holophylla*, and a tall *Tilia miqueliana*, (introduced from eastern China). We explored a series of courtyards, surrounded by temple buildings, each containing at least one golden Buddha, and many small lamps, most of them now lit by electricity. The courtyards were planted with *Prunus, Lagerstroemia, Juniperus chinensis* and many Japanese azalea cultivars.

At the next stop, we explored some impressive modern buildings built in traditional style, and appreciated the terraces planted with *Phyllostachys nigra, Lagerstroemia indica,* groups of *Magnolia liliiflora* and *M. kobus, Pseudocydonia sinensis* and white and pink tree peonies which were just coming into flower.

20 April

Next day we drove to the Chirisan National Park where our guide told us that communist guerrillas had hidden on the Chirisan for nearly five years after the war.

On the way, after a quick lunch of noodles at a wayside restaurant with most dramatic views, we tackled a steep climb up a ridge of the mountain. At this altitude (about 1,100m/3,600ft) hardly any trees were showing leaf, but Kihun helped us to name many of them, including *Staphylea bumalda, Pyrus ussuriensis, Betula dahurica* (with mistletoe on it), *Magnolia sieboldii* and many more. The main cover was of stunted oaks and willows, with some *Taxus cuspidata, Fraxinus chinensis* subsp. *rhynchophylla* and, higher up, *Pinus pumila*. On the way down Kihun also pointed out *Aralia elata. Rhododendron mucronulatum* was in full flower, a lovely deep lavender-pink form, and the woods were full of the enchanting pink *Erythronium japonicum,* with variably spotted leaves.

The next stop down the road was at Sonyu Waterfall, where a Korean family had laid out a ritual feast of cakes and fruit, and were beating an 'hourglass drum'. It was said that they were appeasing evil spirits with a Shamanistic ritual.

Scrambling up past the waterfall, over the boulders, we found *Magnolia sieboldii* clinging to a rock over the river, many young *Stewartia pseudocamellia* var. *koreana* showing the pretty mottled bark, pale stems of *Sapium japonicum, Maackia amurensis, Lindera erythrocarpa* with shaggy bark and many stems, *Corylopsis coreana* Uyeki, *Styrax japonica, Symplocos chinensis* f. *pilosa* (Nakai) Ohwi and many *Prunus serrulata* in flower.

Then we were back in the bus, heading away down the steeply winding road, with granite cliffs above us and deep gorges below, towards Chollipo Arboretum.

21 April

Chollipo is beautiful, and entirely the creation of Mr Min, since 1970. It is situated on the Yellow Sea by a small fishing port and a sandy beach. Although hemmed in by industrial buildings and roads, the surrounding pine woods afford some protection, and the wonderful variety and lushness of the plantings make for an unforgettable experience. Mr Min's favourite genera are perhaps *Magnolia* and *Ilex*, but he is also very interested in native Korean plants, and indeed in all plants. There is an immense variety of species and hybrids here, and a very great number of selected cultivars, especially of *Magnolia*.

The 20 staff are all Koreans, and some have had some period of training or experience in England and America. They maintain 60ha (150 acres) to a very high standard. The altitude range is from sea level to 122m (400ft), and the rainfall about 1000mm (39in). Good composting practice, the lack of late spring frosts and the regular summer rainfall, help to keep the plants in generally superb growing condition. The soil, which is often almost pure sand, with some clay and loam in a few places, is improved as much as possible at planting time, but only the magnolias are regularly fed. They have found a little peat on the site, while constructing a reservoir, and are now allowing all forest debris to remain where it falls in the woodland areas. Previously everything used to be utilised for fuel. They are also planting for wind shelter.

After an exceptionally early spring, some of the magnolias were already over, but there were still plenty to see. An unnamed hybrid *M. acuminata* × *M.* × *soulangeana* makes a splendid tall upright tree, covered in lovely big yellow flowers. *M.* 'Star Wars' also showed up well. At Chollipo, *M. stellata. M. kobus*, and *M.* × *loebneri,* all prefer growing by the waterside, near the two ponds. *M.* × *loebneri* 'Donna', and *M.* 'Royal Flush' are both exceptionally sweetly scented. It was fascinating to see so many in flower, to be able to compare them and to discuss their individual merits.

There is such an immense variety of plants here that it would be foolish to attempt to mention them all. Everything is labelled and recorded. The staff are very happy to send seed lists, and one can only say that anyone planning to plant an arboretum should really come here and see for themselves.

Wandering down the many small paths in the main garden we passed *Pittosporum daphniphylloides, Carpinus coreana* Nakai, which may be more salt resistant than the other species, *Ilex × wandoensis* Dudley et Miller, a natural hybrid discovered growing on Wando Island by Mr Min, *Cornus kousa* 'Pendula', *Sapium japonicum,* notable for splendid autumn colour, *Fagus crenata* var. *multinervis* (Nakai) T. Lee, (R)[2] which is endemic on Ullung Island, *Quercus myrsinifolia, Q. salicina, Morus bombycis* 'Ito', *Berchemia berchemiaefolia* (Mak.) Koidzumi, *Meliosma oldhamii* Miquel, *Taxodium distichum* var. *imbricatum* 'Nutans', in flower, *Stewartia pseudocamellia* Koreana Group with lovely cinnamon-coloured bark, and *S. serrata.* We admired many *Lagerstroemia indica* trees, not yet in leaf or flower, but distinguished for their shape and smooth brown trunks. One especially fine one was 5m high by 7m across (15 × 22ft). There were also some *L. indica × L. fauiei* here. *Michelia* 'Allspice' (*M. doltsopa × M. figo*) had the most delightful golden downy bud calices, and *Melia azedarach* made a big tree. Nearby was *Acer triflorum* with nice shiny bark, *Poupartia fordii* Hemsl and *Cladrastis platycarpa. Acer okomotoanum* Nakai and *A. pseudosieboldianum* subsp. *takesimense* are both endemic to Ullong Island.

22-23 April

In the morning we set out on further exploration of the arboretum. In the Magnolia Hill Area, where a large number of selected forms were planted out in steeply sloping woodland conditions, we noticed *M.* 'Fourteen Karat', (=JG14[Gresham]) only just coming in to flower, and *M.* 'Lilenny' (*M. × soulangeana* 'Lennei' × *M. liliiflora*) was at its best. The charming native *Iris rossii* was in flower. A big *Lagerstroemia fauriei,* distinguished for its red striped trunk, *Chosenia bracteosa* (Turcz) Nakai (*Salix arbutifolia* Pall.) and *Magnolia* 'Darrell Dean' (*M. × veitchii × M.* 'Rustica Rubra') all attracted attention, as did many more magnolias, some as yet unnamed.

Other interesting trees and shrubs included *Lagerstroemia subcostata, Meliosma oldhamii, Exochorda korolkowii,* the rare endemics *Abeliophyllum distichum* (E) and *Celtis koriaensis* (R) and a *Magnolia sieboldii* with pink-tipped tepals which was found by Mr Min in the wild.

After lunch, some of the party went up to Skyline Magnolia, which is somewhat exposed but with lovely views of the sea and the island. Two notably big *Cunninghamia lanceolata* were seen, a large *Magnolia grandiflora* and *M.* 'Yellow Fever' which was much admired for its very striking colour.

We returned to Seoul, and our 32-storey hotel, that night.

24 April

Driving from Seoul, after we had passed through a surreal townscape of tower blocks, interspersed with *Metasequoia glyptostroboides* and *Ginkgo biloba,* we were pleased to see much bigger forest trees than we had so far encountered in Korea.

---

[2] *(E) endangered, (V) vulnerable, (R) rare in the wild.*

At the Kwangnung Arboretum, after a formal but most cordial welcome by the director, Dr Kim Che-chung, we explored this tremendously interesting collection. The Arboretum includes a total of 500ha (1,235 acres) of which 50ha (124 acres) is cultivated ornamentals and 100ha (247 acres) of trial plots of conifers, ornamentals, medicinal plants etc. The rainfall is 1.3m (51in), and the soil is red clay, with sand below and a deep layer of forest litter on top. There were many very big specimens of trees that we had seen elsewhere, and many others not yet encountered. We saw *Castanea crenata*, a native species, widely distributed on hillsides. The nuts are edible, and the wood is used for carvings and roof tiles. Here too were a 100-year-old *Cercidiphyllum japonicum* with two trunks, *Tilia megaphylla* Nakai and *Juglans mandshaurica*, a very tall, straight trunked *Ulmus pumila*, many *Magnolia sieboldii* in bud and a white form of Korean azalea. The many plants in the understorey here included *Convallaria keiskei*, many ferns, and *Disporum sessile*. There was a garden for blind people, with descriptive labels in braille, and a garden for water plants.

We then visited the Forest Museum, which was soon declared to be the best we had seen anywhere in the world. There were giant roots of various species of tree displayed like sculptures, many very well lit photographs, sections of tree trunks showing the bark and the grain, and even the stairs had informative panels set in the side rails. We thanked the Director, who said it was a great pleasure to him to have a visit from fellow plant enthusiasts.

We next arrived at the Hongnung Arboretum, the National Arboretum of Korea, to be greeted by the Forestry Administrator, Mr Lee Bo-Sik.

The survival of so many big trees here is due to the proximity of a royal tomb. The arboretum covers 44ha (110 acres), and contains 2,035 plant species, of which 780 are woody plants. We explored the wooded areas and saw *Acer okomotoanum* Nakai, a very big specimen of *Lindera erythrocarpa* Makino, and *Magnolia sieboldii*, not yet in flower. There was also *Quercus dentata* with very big leaves, *Kalopanax septemlobus* var. *maximowiczii* with deeply cut leaves, *Acer ukurunduense* Trautvetter & Meyer, *Quercus urticifolia* Blume, *Prunus sargentii* with white flowers, *Corylopsis coreana* Uyeki (V), *Broussonetia kazinoki* Siebold var. *humilis*, *Styrax japonica*, *S. obassia*, *Syringa velutina* (Nak.) T.Lee var. *kamibayashii* in flower, *Ilex macropoda*, the dwarf and spreading *Thuja koraiensis* and *Larix gmelinii* var. *principis-ruprechtii*. The overhead cover was mainly *Quercus* and *Pinus densiflora*.

Rain descended as we returned to Seoul, and the streets were lined with gaily coloured umbrellas, covering the market stalls.

25 April

Dr Kim Yong-Dok, the distinguished physicist, accompanied us for part of this day. He was most informative on all sorts of interesting subjects, and particularly helpful on the design of the traditional Korean garden. He explained that a natural style is combined with orderliness, according to the Yin (dark) and Yang (light) Taoist and Confucianist principles.

Our next visit was to a reconstruction of a traditional Korean garden which was only completed in June 1997. Great numbers of very tall, some 10m (30ft), trees were successfully transplanted here. We passed through a gate between cobb walls inset with tiles in patterns, to a bamboo grove, which represents the dark, or earthly forces, and came through to where the water and bright flowers represent the light, or heavenly forces. Beside a pool there was a pavilion sited for meditation. The reflections in the water, the shapes of the rocks and the colours, are all designed to provoke pleasing thoughts. The view of a much larger lake, below the garden, and also the wooded hill beyond, are all considered as part of the design.

26 April

As we drove up the valleys, going east from Seoul, the road winding among the hills, we saw a beautiful range of shades of green foliage. Here the trees were bigger, and always mixed deciduous and conifers, with cherry, pear and peach blossom. There had been much clear felling and replanting in vertical rows. *Pinus densiflora* was planted lower down and *P. koraiensis* higher up.

We came to Woljong-sa Temple, one of the most famous in Korea. Here were many 100-year-old *Abies holophylla* while *Forsythia* and *R. schlippenbachii* were still in flower at this higher altitude.

At a later stop, a short excursion over a stony river took us among *Acer mono, Betula schmidtii* Regel, *Fraxinus chinensis* subsp. *rhyncophylla, Styrax obassia,* a 12m (40ft) tall *Cornus controversa, Magnolia*

sieboldii, Betula dahurica close to the river, and *B. ermanii* at 14m (46ft) tall and showing v-shaped cuts. These cuts are made to drain the sap which is used as a medicinal drink. There were also many interesting herbaceous plants and ferns, and the leaves of *Erythronium japonicum,* but the flowers were well over.

Our destination was the Soraksan National Park. Soraksan is a very popular resort for Koreans.

27 April

We awoke to bright sunshine, lighting up the rosy pink granite mountain peaks, here piercing the green mantle of unfolding forest leaves. One or two patches of snow still lay in the shaded gullies.

We took the cable car up the mountain to about 1,000m (3,300ft) above sea level and scrambled up from there. The trees, mainly *Quercus* and *Acer* with some *Pinus densiflora* and *Abies koreana,* were stunted. We saw *Rhododendron schlippenbachii* in flower, *R. mucronulatum* just going over, *Viburnum wrightii* which is similar to *V. dilatatum,* and *Forsythia ovata.* Chipmunks were seen and the Korean edelweiss, *Leontopodium coreanum* Nakai, found. The views to still higher mountains were superb.

After descending we followed Kihun up beside the river. He has an insatiable craving for more plants, and we saw many *Styrax obassia* just coming into flower. The tree cover was mostly pines and oaks, with few trees of any size. However, there were many seedlings. Many trees were labelled and we saw *Syringa reticulata* subsp. *amurensis, Lindera obtusiloba* with soft felted leaves, *Quercus mongolica, Malus baccata* var. *mandschurica* with big white flowers, *Picrasma quassioides, Diospyros lotus, Magnolia sieboldii* full of flower bud, *Acer truncatum, Alnus hirsuta, Aristolochia manshuriensis* Komarov, *Lilium tigrinum* but not in flower, *Hovenia dulcis, Deutzia* and a giant *Actinidia arguta*, at least 30m (100ft) long and 25cm (10in) in circumference.

28 April

Our final day was spent in the coach, but we enjoyed a most scenic drive through the Soraksan National Park, following the river, and seeing wisteria naturalised on the rocks at the side of the road. We passed lakes and some smooth, pink, granite, dome-shaped hills, contrasting with the sharp crags to be seen from the other side of the bus. Korean azalea was flowering among the boulders on the river banks.

At the Yongmunsa Temple we were promised a very special treat and, after a brisk uphill walk, we came to the most glorious *Ginkgo biloba* tree in front of the temple, at the stream's edge. It was a wonderful sight, soaring to more than 60m (200ft) and 14m (46ft) in circumference, fully clad in lovely greenery and plainly in the best of health. It is estimated to be over 1000 years old and is a female tree.

At our final dinner that night, we thanked Mr Min, our kind host, who had invited us all to Korea, and who had given us such a wonderful experience of his most beautiful country, and Mr Song Kihun, who had guided us so ably and enthusiastically through such a wide variety of plant species, many of them previously unknown to us.

Acknowledgements

My special thanks to Mr Song Kihun, for much checking and correcting, and to my husband, for the map.

References

Hillier Manual of Trees and Shrubs, The. 6th Edition (1996). David and Charles, Devon.

Krussman's Manual of Cultivated Broadleaved Trees and Shrubs (1984). B T Batsford, London.

MABBERLEY, D J (1997). *The Plant Book.* 2nd ed. Cambridge University Press, Cambridge.

TAE-WOOK, PROF. KIM (1994). *Woody Plants of Korea.* Kyohak Publishing Co. Ltd, Seoul, Korea.

VAN GELDEREN, D M, DE JONG, P C, OTTERDOOM, H J (1994). *Maples of the World.* Timber Press, USA.

Anne Boscawen is a member of the Group. The family garden, High Beeches at Handcross, Sussex, contains a celebrated collection of trees and woody plants

CAMELLIA FLOWER BLIGHT

HERB SHORT

When an Italian visitor at last year's Royal Horticultural Society London Flower Show in March discovered that there was an impossibly long waiting list for a recently introduced camellia, she responded, 'Well, I couldn't take one back anyway because you English have this horrible disease.'

The 'horrible disease' is *Ciborinia camelliae* Kohn – camellia flower, or petal, blight. Although it does not affect the health of the camellia plant, it turns the flowers brown in a matter of a few days, often as the buds open. And there is no known cure.

Two years ago it was identified, through laboratory analysis by the Central Science Laboratory of the Ministry of Agriculture, Fisheries and Food (MAFF), as being in Cornwall and as far east as the Southampton area.

Last year, at the RHS March show, flower blight symptoms were visible on 20 blooms during the first day of the camellia competition and by the second day, most of those blooms had turned almost completely brown. There was at least one plant on an exhibitor's stand with flower blight symptoms and my wife and I found three blooms with flower blight on a bush of *C.* × *williamsii* 'Jury's Yellow' in our south London garden late last spring – an indication that the disease is not confined to the South-West.

However, camellia flower blight is far from being an English disease. In fact, England is merely one of the most recent places where the disease has been identified and Australia is probably the only major camellia growing country where it has not been discovered.

Yet flower blight is a disease that some countries and individual gardeners are reluctant, or even unwilling, to admit they have – like that deep family secret locked in the room at the top of the dark stairs in those 1930s black-and-white horror films. For instance, last year the UK Region of the International Camellia Society asked its more than 350 members to take part in a survey of flower blight and report any findings of it. Only one member responded.

The disease was first reported in literature in Japan in 1919 by K Hara, and originally called *Sclerotinia camelliae* Hara. In 1938, it was found at the nursery of a Japanese-American in California. By 1950, it had travelled more than 3,200km (2,000 miles), crossing mountains and desert and was infecting camellias in the Deep South of Louisiana. It rapidly spread up the US east coast as far north as Virginia, where it was apparently halted by the cold winters.

That was the way things stood for 50 years. Then, in the early 1990s, flower blight suddenly appeared in the Wellington area in New Zealand. By 1999, it was reported as far north as Auckland and also found to be well established in the South Island.

Meanwhile, rumours had it in Europe. These have been confirmed, although not always officially, over the past two years, with flower blight identified in the Channel Islands, France, Germany, Italy, Portugal, Spain and Switzerland, in addition to England.

Actually, the disease may have been in Europe longer than suspected, perhaps held in check by unfavourable weather conditions until the recent mild winters, or simply ignored or unrecognised. Without close examination, the browning of blooms is easily dismissed as frost damage, old age or *botrytis*. Even with close examination, flower blight can sometimes be difficult to identify.

Moreover, there seemed to be no reason to examine brown and weathered old blooms that closely. Flower blight was a disease we were confident we did not have because the British weather was just too mean and nasty for it, and there were regulations in place restricting imports from outside the European Community.

Rules on blight

At the UK's request in 1992, an EC Plant Health Directive relating to camellia flower blight was adopted. The UK equivalent, Plant Health Great Britain Order of 1993, states that camellia imports must be accompanied by 'an official statement that the plants originate in areas free from *Ciborinia camelliae* Kohn, or no symptoms have been observed on plants in flower in the place of production since the beginning of the last complete cycle of vegetation.'

Elsewhere, rules have been in effect for a number of years. For instance, Nuccio's Nurseries in Altadena, California, perhaps the most famous camellia nursery in the world, has shipped bare-root camellias to several states and to foreign countries to eliminate flower blight being carried in the soil. Their catalogue includes the statement, 'All states and countries requiring bare-root shipment of Camellias . . . [must have plants] inspected and certified by the Los Angeles County Dept. of Agriculture'.

Within the past few years, Nuccio's has further restricted shipments to only scions with no flower buds to a number of countries, including the UK.

But rules are difficult to enforce. Plant fanatics easily find ways to circumvent them. Even those with the required phytosanitary certificates for their imports sometimes meet with indifference at inspection points. It now seems likely that rules will change. How, it remains to be seen.

Martin Ward of MAFF's Plant Health Division, says, 'The UK took the lead in 1993 in getting EC-wide measures agreed against the introduction to Europe of camellia flower blight. However, information received in 1998 suggests that the disease had become established in some areas. At our request, the Commission asked all Member States to carry out surveys for the disease. We have now asked the EC's Plant

Health Committee to consider, in light of the results of those surveys, whether quarantine measures are still appropriate.'

Living with blight

Meanwhile, gardeners with camellias must learn to live with camellia flower blight. This means learning to recognise it and taking steps to keep it out of their gardens – or at least keep it in check.

Flower blight first appears as tiny brown pinpoints on the camellia petals, the result of ascospores (fungal seeds) landing and germinating. The infection spreads as a fungal mycelium within the petal tissue to the base of the flower, then works its way back outward.

The growing mycelium forms asexual spores (microconidia), which are sterile and cannot spread flower blight to other flowers or to other plants, as is common with other fungal diseases. This is one of the few fortunate things about this most flower-disfiguring disease.

In addition to turning brown, flowers usually, although not always, feel slimy. Often the veins of the petals result in a wood-grain effect – a sign, but not a foolproof one, that a bloom may be infected with flower blight.

Positive identification is made by removing the sepals at the base of the bloom. A solid white ring of fungus around the base of the flower is the trademark of flower blight (see Fig. 9).

Often this hyphae ring is smooth, thick and brilliant white. But in this imperfect world, the ring may be grey-white and somewhat ill-defined, making it difficult to tell for certain that it is flower blight and not the *botrytis* fungus, which is grey and usually fuzzy, or *Penicillium*, a clear grey-blue fuzz, which also attacks the ovary. White flowers can add a bit of uncertainty to ring identification, of course, because their base is white from the start.

At this point, the infected bloom should be destroyed, either by boiling it or disposing of it in a secure heavy-duty rubbish bag.

It is also at this point that fungal energy produces sclerotia at the base of the flower. The area surrounding the white ring first begins to harden and then one large, brown-to-black sclerotium, or several smaller sclerotia form. Depending on the temperature, this is usually only two to three weeks after the brown spots first appear on the petals.

The infected flower falls to the ground and rots, leaving the sclerotia to winter on, or just under, the ground. Because of their size and colour, they are difficult to detect, particularly on ground that has been mulched (see Fig. 10).

In late winter or early spring, the sclerotia germinate, sending up fungal stipes, which form the fruiting structures, the apothecia. These structures can vary in size from a few millimetres to a centimetre or more in diameter. The larger ones are about the diameter of a 10p coin. Their appearance is that of a small, tan, saucer-shaped mushroom (see Fig. 11).

After a few days, spores within the mushroom mature and are forcibly ejected *en masse*, early in the morning when the dew is drying. They are quickly picked up by even a slight breeze. Although they do not survive for long, unless they land on a camellia flower, they can be carried in a viable state for at least a mile. Reportedly, in one instance in New Zealand, they have blown more than 19km (12 miles) across a body of water and infected camellias on the other side.

The numbers are frightening. The same mushroom can eject more than 1 million spores at a time for one to two weeks, while the same sclerotium can continue to produce new mushrooms for several weeks.

Cool, cloudy, damp weather provides the ideal conditions for spore formation, release and survival. The fungus grows best when temperatures are 10-18°C (50-64°F). Few sclerotia germinate to produce spores when there has been no rain for at least 10 days. But sclerotia can remain viable in or on the ground for at least four years.

Luther W Baxter, Jr, Professor Emeritus, Department of Plant Pathology and Physiology, Clemson University in Clemson, South Carolina, has spent a lifetime attempting to find a truly effective, practical cure for flower blight. He says, 'It can probably be stated with reasonable accuracy that the fungus can survive wherever camellias can be grown.'

However, there are no reported cases of sclerotia germinating outdoors north of Virginia in the US, in areas where, although spring conditions might seem favourable, winter temperatures can drop to −18°C (0°F) or below for several days at a time.

Still, the sclerotia do seem to need a cooling-off period. Once the spring camellia season is over, they do not germinate until the following year, which in warmer climates can mean as early as late December. This spares autumn-blooming species, such as *C. sasanqua*, and cold-hardy hybrids from attack.

Researchers at Massey University, Palmerston North, New Zealand, have carried out preliminary screening showing that *C. sasanqua* varieties are susceptible to the disease, as are *C. japonica*, *C. reticulata*, *C. saluenensis*, *C. pitardii* and hybrids between them.

Peter Long, Senior Lecturer in Plant Pathology at Massey, reported at the 1999 International Camellia Congress in Miyazaki, Japan, that various species – *C. yunnanensis*, *C. forrestii*, *C. grijsii*, *C. lutchuensis*, *C. transnokoensis* and *C. yuhsienensis* – show some resistance. A Massey graduate student, Christine Taylor, is continuing work on species resistance with the aid of the New Zealand Camellia Memorial Trust and Descanso Gardens and Huntington Botanical Gardens in the US.

No Cure

So far, no fungicidal treatment of flowers or soil has been sufficiently effective on a practical basis and placing black plastic on the soil during the camellia flowering season has physical limitations. There are just too many sclerotia, apothecia and spores.

The only answer for the camellia grower at this point is to practice clean gardening. All brown flowers on the ground or still on the plant should be removed and blighted flowers boiled or disposed of in a secure heavy-duty plastic bag. The more difficult to find sclerotia and apothecia, should be disposed of in the same way.

For estates and large gardens, the task may be impossible. In the average garden, clean gardening is not only possible, but is already being done – for instance, many gardeners deadhead roses. In the case of camellias, it merely means working when the weather may not be as friendly.

My wife and I practiced clean gardening last year with 50 camellias – some in the ground, some in pots, and some as old as 15 years. Only three blighted flowers and no sclerotia or apothecia were found. Two of the blooms were retained and developed sclerotia.

Some gardeners will argue that unless everyone does it, clean gardening will not work. Greg Davis, a vice-president of the International Camellia Society living in a major camellia growing area in Houston, Texas, practices clean gardening and has no trouble with flower blight. On the other hand, a friend living a number of miles away has given up competing in camellia shows because his camellias turn brown as they open.

The flowers of newly purchased camellias should be examined for flower blight. It is safer to simply remove all flowers and flower buds at the time of purchase. The soil in the container should be monitored for sclerotia and apothecia at least for one complete growth cycle. If a new plant is to be kept in a container, the top one-half inch of soil can be carefully removed. If a new purchase is to be planted immediately, it can be bare-rooted and the soil disposed of in a secure, heavy-duty plastic bag. Bare-rooting can be a bit risky, however, and probably should not be attempted with reticulatas, which tend to be delicate and temperamental.

Camellias have spoiled gardeners because they have been low-maintenance plants. However, we have a friend who has been saying for years that he is disappointed with camellias because they are always filled with unsightly brown flowers. His observations perhaps indicate that, for most gardeners, they have been no-maintenance plants. Camellias deserve better, whether the unsightly brown is just the weather – or flower blight.

References

BAXTER, L W Jr, (1995). Camellia Flower Blight in the USA. *International Camellia Journal* **27**: 56-59.

COOPER, K, MANNING M, FULLERTON B, (1997). Camellia Flower Blight. *International Camellia Journal* **29**: 102-08.

LONG, P, TAYLOR, C, (1999). Research on Camellia Flower Blight in New Zealand. *International Camellia Journal* **31**: 99-102.

PEPER, K, (1999). Die Braunfäulen der Kamelienblüte: *Ciborinia camelliae* Kohn....*die Kamelie* **1**: 1-23. www.kamelien.de

SHORT, H, (1995). A Hard Look at Flower Blight. *International Camellia Journal* **27**: 52-53.

TAYLOR, C, (2000). Petal Blight Research. *The Camellia Review* **61 (3)**: 4-5.

Herb Short is Editor of the International Camellia Journal

Where Have All the Rhododendrons Gone?

Peter Cox

It is strange that rhododendron societies the world over are having problems in keeping up their membership, as I feel that our problems in the UK are not necessarily the same as elsewhere. It could be that it is just a case of a genus falling out of favour, as so many have done over the centuries. As has rightly been pointed out, conifers have also dropped off in popularity. It so happens that in this country both rhododendrons and conifers have suffered bad publicity of late. In the case of rhododendrons it has been due to *R. ponticum* being referred to generically as 'rhododendrons', and not just as one rogue species, and with conifers it has been (as we all know) due to × *Cupressocyparis leylandii*. It is also probably true that many people may think that rhododendrons are only for large gardens and for the rich landowner. But none of these points should really apply in North America, New Zealand, etc. There are certainly difficulties over planting container grown rhododendrons, to which John Bond alluded in his Chairman's Foreword to the 2000 Year Book, which would certainly apply equally in other countries.

There are various other factors that perhaps add up to the reduction in interest. Plants reverting to *R. ponticum* has always been a difficult problem to overcome and a few unscrupulous nurserymen who still use it as an understock on grafted plants certainly do not help our cause.

Global warming may have only come to the fore quite recently, but we have been having quite early springs, followed by late damaging frosts for the great majority of the last 20 years – 1998 and 1999 were particularly devastating and, apart from 1998 and 2000, our summers have been getting drier, sometimes disastrously so.

Diseases and pests are another factor. We all used to think that our rhododendrons were comparatively trouble free, but in recent years powdery mildew has appeared and honey fungus, *Phytophthora*, galls and rust seem to be getting worse. Most people now suffer to a greater or lesser extent from weevils.

Other, perhaps lesser factors, are the anti peat lobby; unsatisfactory new American hybrids, particularly those from microprops where the plant has been altered in some detrimental way; a lack of commercial rhododendron exhibits at shows; horticultural journalists that seem to be anti-rhododendron, either disparaging or ignoring them; the present run of gardening programmes on television that seem to copy each other; and younger gardeners who seem to dislike getting their hands dirty and are impatient for instant results, something that most larger rhododendron species just will not give.

The average age of members of rhododendron societies, especially those who attend meetings and go on garden tours, plus the few that are willing to sit on committees, seems to get older and older. Will future retired people come into the fold? And yet, here at Glendoick, we have sold out our *Encyclopedia of Rhododendron Species* much quicker than we expected, and now we wish we had another 500 printed. Has this book led to an increase in our sales of species? I do not think so. We are nevertheless getting it reprinted.

What can we do to improve matters? Of the younger generation, the likes of David Millais and Kenneth Cox try their best, but they are probably only speaking to the converted anyway. People have plenty of opportunities to see rhododendrons these days, with all the gardens that are open to the public, but the trouble may be that people cannot imagine transferring what they observe in these, mostly large, gardens to their own patch. Perhaps even the mere fact that these gardens are now so readily available for viewing makes growing the plants themselves unnecessary.

Peter Cox is well known as a breeder of rhododendrons, a plant hunter and as the author of many books about the genus Rhododendron. *He is a director of Glendoick Gardens Ltd, the rhododendron garden and nursery near Perth, Scotland*

SHERINGHAM PARK - A FURTHER 50 YEARS

KEITH ZEALAND

The RHS *Rhododendron Year Book* of 1951–2 included a short article describing the woods on the Sheringham Estate, written by the owner Mr Thomas Upcher. These few paragraphs detailed the growing conditions and history of his collection of rhododendrons, camellias and magnolias dated from the mid-1800s. The plants listed included 65 species of rhododendron, of which at least 12 were a result of Mr Upcher's grandfather being involved in the Veitchian expeditions of E H Wilson in the early years of the last century. These include large specimens of *R. calophytum*, *R. sutchuenense*, *R. floribundum* and *R. praevernum*. Among those not attributed to Wilson, but growing in the same areas, are *R. rex* subsp. *fictolacteum*, *R. laxiflorum* and *R. niveum*, the latter noted as being one of Hooker's introductions.

It is important to observe Mr Upcher's emphatic dislike of the term 'woodland garden'. He used simply 'the woods' when referring to his 20-ha (50-acre) site. The approach to the house is flanked on both sides with old hardy hybrid rhododendrons forming dense cover for nearly three-quarters of its length – one mile in total. Magnificent old oaks and Scots pines barely dominate an often continuous thicket of rhododendrons, several hectares of which

can only be viewed from the two towers erected specifically for the purpose – but what views they are (see Fig. 21).

Visiting expert gardeners and 'rhodophiles' first of all find it difficult to believe the extent and diversity of the collection, it being far from the usual location (and climate) of such gardens in Britain. Indeed several have gone away in disbelief, unable to fathom how the plants remain in such good health on less than 60cm (24in) of rainfall per year. In addition, the soils are very variable, being mostly sand and gravels and fairly acidic although often with great chunks of chalk held in suspension, having been scraped off the underlying strata by glaciers thousands of years ago. Thus it is common to see privet and spindle shrubs growing alongside rhododendrons, yet impossible to grow lime-hating plants in the nearby village without great difficulty.

Apart from the rhododendrons there are around 15 kinds of magnolia, including a 15m plus (50ft) *M. campbellii* subsp. *mollicomata*, *M. sieboldii* and *M. sprengeri* var. *diva*. Of the 50-odd other genera represented at Sheringham, a few stand out particularly, with *Eucryphia* × *nymansensis* being the odd one out as it is usually the only plant flowering in the garden during late summer. But among the others, *Crinodendron hookerianum, Pseudolarix amabilis* and *Nyssa sylvatica* appear alongside massive *Pieris formosa* var. *forrestii* (see Fig. 19) and a *Halesia monticola* which is surely among the tallest in the country. Some plants are in obvious decline, including the very popular *Davidia involucrata*, now rapidly turning to dead wood, and a *Dipelta* in pitiful condition, although apparently once of huge proportions.

There is no doubt, though, that most visitors come at the end of May and early June to see the brilliant spectacle of hundreds of old hardy hybrids in full bloom. Mr Upcher listed over 30 varieties in his article as being of special note of which most still grow at Sheringham, many others having been added by him over the years. Although some, such as *R.* 'Christmas Cheer' and *R.* 'Nobleanum Venustum' appear as early as January, the high season is crowned with such favourites as *R.* 'Doncaster', *R.* 'Sappho', *R.* 'Gomer Waterer', *R.* 'Brittania' (see Fig. 20), *R.* 'Purple Splendour', *R.* 'Mother of Pearl' and so on. Hybrids of *R. × loderi*, *r. souliei* and *R. griersonianum* are scattered throughout, although quite a lot still await a visit from someone with the expertise to determine their names. The actual number of varieties is unknown, due partly to Mr Upcher's fondness for raising and planting out his homegrown seedlings.

It was when he died, in 1986, that the National Trust purchased the estate, with the assistance of the late owner's trustees. The prime reason for the acquisition was to protect the historic landscape park and sea views, designed by Humphry Repton

and declared by him to be his 'most favourite work'. The wild garden was also an important feature of the property and initially a care and maintenance regime was implemented, for in the first few years the greatest effort was directed towards making the property suitable for year-round access by visitors.

When attention turned to the plants, it quickly became apparent that *R. ponticum* was steadily throttling much of the diversity in the collection, and had been for many decades. Mr Upcher had rightly pointed out that it needed to be restrained ruthlessly, but its pernicious creeping habit can be deceptive. As a striking example of the problem, although Mr Upcher ended his 1951 article with a hope that his recently ordered *R. macabeanum* would survive the cold and wind at Sheringham, it took three years of searching to find this distinctive plant, by then 40 years old. *R. ponticum* had filled every gap except regularly used paths, much of it issuing from the rootstock grafts of more than 50 years ago. Clearly, drastic measures were needed.

A plan of campaign was approved by the National Trust's Gardens Panel. The plan detailed the need for survey and cataloguing, swiftly followed by emergency remedial work and then implementation of a longer term work programme, with the money coming from the Trust's Gardens Fund. This fund is largely made up of income from the National Gardens Scheme, for which the Trust is an active fundraiser. The grant was supplemented by money raised on the property, and it paid for temporary staff and the equipment needed to work in the depths of a hillside jungle. The terrain at Sheringham, to the newcomer, is a quite unexpected feature of the 'flat' county of Norfolk.

In the course of the work, many 'lost' specimens came to light more or less intact, but it was clear that others had succumbed, including a *R. ambiguum* described in 1951 as almost 6m (20ft) tall. The largest one discovered was just a little over 2m (6ft) high. Other species that Mr Upcher described in the plural were found in the singular. Not surprisingly perhaps, an entire suite of smaller species including *R. calostrotum* subsp. *keleticum*, *R. impeditum* and *R. pemakoense* was absent.

The whole situation was exacerbated by the gales of 1987 and 1991 when large falling trees absolutely flattened a 50m (165ft) long bank of *R. decorum* and *R. fortunei* hybrids, as well as many individual specimens and areas of single variety plantings. The work did succeed, though, in rediscovering 50 of the 65 species listed by Mr Upcher, plus many of the hybrids and other plants put in since the 1950s. Even now, eight years on, new finds occasionally turn up among the native trees, the most recent being a *Styrax* and a *Magnolia*.

Since the early days of the National Trust's ownership, the popularity of the estate with visitors has been such that a second full-time member of staff has been taken on, and this has allowed a developmental stage to evolve. New plantings have taken place and an important process of propagating the old specimens can begin, particularly of the best forms of commoner subjects, or of those original plants now in recession or unobtainable.

New areas have been identified for expansion within the site, and control of *R. ponticum* continues, making space for new plants and new stock from recent collecting trips (when it is offered). This is an exciting prospect, but it is important to keep ambition within the bounds of practical achievement. Mr Upcher listed the rabbit as his chief enemy in those pre-myxomatosis days and while that is no longer relevant, the diminutive muntjac deer are beginning to nibble at insufficiently protected young plants. Luckily, they do not gnaw like rabbits, though they sometimes rub off bark and scrape around the roots. The old enemies of bracken and bramble remain, however. It has been suggested, also, that too-efficient removal of *R. ponticum* could alter the microclimate enough to threaten the general growing conditions, which must be marginal in this place. So a balance has to be struck, though in the wider estate wholesale eradication is the aim to protect native species living in the 200ha (500 acres) of woodland.

Nevertheless, if the effects of global warming do not radically alter the environment in north Norfolk, the woods at Sheringham will remain an excellent place to see rhododendrons, old and new, for many decades to come.

Reference

UPCHER, THOMAS (1951). Rhododendrons in East Anglia – Sheringham Park. *The Rhododendron Year Book 1951-2*. The Royal Horticultural Society. London.

Keith Zealand is Head Warden at the National Trust's Sheringham Park, Norfolk

RETICULATA CAMELLIAS IN MID SUSSEX

JOHN HILLIARD

One grows reticulata camellias from China for much the same combination of reasons that one may keep Tragopan pheasants from the Himalayas – they are the most magnificent of their kind, they demand special attention and they amply reward the care they are given. This philosophy does not spring from mature rationalisation but is rather the result of 30-odd years of strenuous, sustained and largely unsuccessful effort to grow species rhododendrons in a small patch of Weald clay. The rhododendrons have, for the most part, dwindled away, while camellias, planted casually and indiscriminately, have flourished. Delighted with this adventitious success I decided to have a small adventure with reticulatas. My first plant, which amazingly I still have, was *C. reticulata* 'William Hertrich'. I now have a few more and offer some observations on trying to grow these great plants with minimal shelter but without heat.

Given the conditions of a small town garden, I began inevitably with containers. This avenue proved, more or less, a dead end and I am still not quite sure why. Trehane's had some magnificent specimens in large, fairly shallow pots but nearly all my plants eventually showed signs of distress. There was nothing obviously life-threaten-

ing but the roots, fleshier than those of japonicas, seemed desperate to get down to the bottom of the pot. It may be relevant that last year I found my 'Mouchang' seedlings flopping in their new growth even though they were in shade and damp. More watering did not help but left standing in a saucer of water they stopped wilting. Ailing mature plants if caught in time and planted out recovered with remarkable rapidity. Though I readily admit the likelihood of pilot error, it seems possible that reticulatas have an even stronger urge than japonicas to go deep. My experience is that heavy Weald clay beneath a foot or so of loam is ideal for camellias; once established they seem indifferent to prolonged drought while all around are suffering. Trying to transplant them out of the clay, however, calls for great effort and optimism.

Having, thus, to abandon the project of reticulatas in containers but still set on growing them, I then had to consider what shelter would be needed in the open ground. I had already tried a couple of seedlings outside and without shelter, or indeed any special attention, but they had dwindled into decay. I began with small greenhouses but reticulatas are trees and anything short of 2m (6ft) for a flourishing plant is unfitting. I next tried a plastic tunnel which friends and I put up ourselves – just. The plants flourished in the enclosed atmosphere but, of course, the sloping sides were a practical and aesthetic handicap. I had already approached one of the major firms for a decent-sized glasshouse but they required access for an articulated lorry which was out of the question for what had now become a jungle, precluding the use even of a wheelbarrow.

The solution was a Metapost framework and a very large Visqueen sheet recommended and supplied by Fargro. This gives us a height of 2.2m (7ft): not enough but workable. The plants are flourishing even though rolling up the plastic at either end provides the only ventilation. Of course it gets pretty hot in the summer and I attempted to rig up some makeshift shading. Now I rely on the grime of the aging Visqueen. The house is kept humid by spraying but hardly ever ground watered. There is no heating and no extra protection, such as horticultural fleece, provided, and the only damage from cold has been to the very young growth from the severe and late frost in 1999.

This experience prompts the obvious question. Do we need to bother with shelter at all? The answer must lie in experiment and indeed I have no other option since the Visqueen house is now as much of a jungle as the rest of the garden. We enjoy, generally, pretty favourable conditions for the experiment with reticulatas without shelter. Crawley provides a few degrees extra warmth compared with the open country, the jungle provides both canopy and protection from wind and recent winters have been kind.

We already have some experiments in hand although the results are so far inconclusive. 'Francie L.', 'Miss Tulare' and 'Else Dryden' are, up until now, as good outside as under cover. 'Mandalay Queen' (see Fig. 17), 'Clifford Parks' and 'Royalty' look well but have no flower buds while 'Arbutus Gum' has struggled for years and is now under plastic. Perhaps the plastic offers just that small buffer against the weather that some kinds or some individual plants welcome or need.

The only feeding in the shelter has been an annual sprinkle of Vitax but the whole area is well mulched. The basis of the mulch is oak leaves from our own and neighbours' gardens supplemented by spent hops from a friendly local brewery, and bracken mulch bought from Ashdown Forest Conservation. A remarkable, and most welcome, feature of the shelter is the absence of pests. There is the occasional scale or black fly, which riot in the glasshouses, and we grow wild garlic to ward off black fly.

The drawback for the avid collector – one who always has as much as he needs but never as much as he wants – is the difficulty of acquiring anything beyond one or two pretty common kinds. Since I have comparative rarities like 'Loretta Feathers' (see Fig. 16), 'Pharoah' and 'Hody Wilson' I have naturally tried my best to propagate them from cuttings using every kind of medium, including Yakuma from Japan. The failure has been total and grafting by some expert acquaintances has been no more successful. My latest effort has been to enlist the aid of a friend and expert John

Mead, who made half a dozen air layers. My only path to success has been through seed. One of my favourites, 'Mouchang' (see Fig. 18), regularly sets seed and the first seedlings have flowered this year when four years old. Two of them are as good as, though different from, 'Mouchang' itself. I put the seed in a glass jar of moist peat in the airing cupboard and they soon germinate and form a snaking 7.5cm (3in) tap root. I have the odd younger seedling from 'Loretta Feathers' and 'Hody Wilson'.

The plants that I have found especially attractive are 'K. O. Hester', 'Overture', 'Miss Tulare', 'Debut', 'Lila Naff', 'Lasca Beauty' and 'Otto Hopfer'. Triumphs in the open air have been 'Satan's Robe' and 'Salutation'. There are some hybrids that are not to my taste for, at least here, they carry no characteristics of *C. reticulata*; 'Black Lace' springs to mind. There are however others, like 'Aztec' and 'San Marino' that I would dearly love to try and I am investigating possible suppliers from nurseries in Italy and Switzerland. Meanwhile I fervently recommend reticulatas for enthusiasts who will accept nothing but the top of the tree – but avoid Tragopan pheasants who find the flowers a tasty if unsustaining snack.

John Hilliard is a member of the Group and Chairman of the South East Branch

Vincent Square Rhododendron Competitions – Why aren't we interested?

Brian Wright

The millennium rhododendron competitions – the early one in March and the main one in April – were supported by only six entrants. Or to put it more pointedly, under one percent of the total UK membership of the Rhododendron, Camellia and Magnolia Group; in fact there were probably three times as many judges as contestants, a ratio which further throws such woeful support into depressingly sharp focus.

The competitions schedule a total of 80 classes, broadly divided into species and hybrids. Within these definitions are classes for trusses, sprays, large-leafed rhododendrons, alpines, lepidotes, elepidotes, tender types, vireyas etc. Indeed, enough classes to give every rhododendron grower an opportunity to compete.

Apart from opportunity, the classes also offer incentives: cash prizes which, over the two competitions, total £827.50 and six prestigious and historical trophies – some of which are illustrated on p.44.

Like most competitions, there are rules (the RHS call them regulations and they are published in the annual Competition Schedule), judges (experienced rhododendron people) and stewards to help entrants stage their entries. From hereafter, however, the events become much more than competitions, they become public displays. Given this situation, it is incumbent upon the Group membership to produce the very best show of rhododendrons that it can. Since it has not been doing so for a number of years now, an excellent opportunity is being lost to advertise and promote the genus and, indeed, the Group itself. To find support a little more forthcoming, one has to go back to 1995 when 14 competitors took part in the main rhododendron competition. In the 70s and 80s, it was the norm for 30 or more contestants to exhibit and produce, in the RHS New Hall, a great swathe of colour and an exciting buzz of interest and enthusiasm. In those days, the competitions not only made an impressive rhododendron statement but did what all worthwhile specialist events should do:

- draw together enthusiasts from many parts of the country to share a common interest;
- exhibit the good, the new and the rare;
- offer an inspiring sense of occasion.

Of course, gardening times have changed and some of the larger and more illustrious names that graced the show benches with their blooms either no longer exist, have diminished resources or priorities that are now somewhat removed from rhododendrons. This decline in itself, however, cannot wholly excuse the current embarrassingly poor showing at Vincent Square. Certainly the camellia competitions do not appear to be suffering the same blight, as these are as keenly contested as ever. And better supported rhododendron shows are being seen in Scotland and Cornwall and where certain Group Branches have organised their own events. So why then aren't we doing better in London.

I am sure that we all have our views on what's going wrong and these might cover:

• a certain personal and pervading diffidence about showing;
• the chore of transporting blooms to London;
• Westminster's horrendous and very expensive parking regulations;
• the modest publicity given to the competitions;

• the paltry publicity given to the prizewinners – a facility that, if improved, could greatly benefit larger gardens open to the public;
• a feeling that more trophies could be awarded, with medals and replicas to keep instead of just silverware to borrow annually;
• judging criteria (not laid down in writing) which perhaps should be reviewed and updated.

But views are one thing and knowing why the competitions do not attract better support quite another. Surely it is time for the RHS Rhododendron, Camellia and Magnolia Group management to conduct a considered survey among its members to discover precisely why there is a current reluctance to show. For it is only by knowing why that we can properly address the situation.

Brian Wright is a member of the group. He competes regularly with success at the London Flower Shows and some years ago initiated the Group's South East Branch's Spring Competition, now a well supported annual event

THE COMPETITIONS' SILVERWARE

Over the years, the competitions' silverware (six prestigious and historical trophies) have been won by some of the most famous names in gardening. The four shown here are The McLaren Challenge Cup, The Loder Challenge Cup, The Crosfield Challenge Cup and the newest trophy, The Alan Hardy Challenge Salver.

The two not shown are The Lionel de Rothschild Challenge Cup, awarded at the Main Rhododendron Competition for the six best species, and The Roza Stevenson Challenge Cup, also awarded at that event for the best single species spray.

The McLaren Challenge Cup awarded at the Main Competition for the best single species truss

The Loder Challenge Cup awarded at the Main Competition for the best single hybrid truss

The Crosfield Challenge Cup awarded at the Main Competition for the best three hybrids bred and raised in the garden of the contestant

The Alan Hardy Challenge Salver awarded for the first time last year at the Early Competition to the entrant amassing the highest points aggregate across all classes

RHODODENDRONS AND OTHER PLANTS IN TIBET'S TSARI VALLEY

PHILIP EVANS

The Tsari chu, as its Tibetan epithet signifies, is a small river. It rises in the southern watershed of the Himalaya of south-east Tibet, and runs eastwards down to and across the Indian border, which at this point lies in an almost north-south direction. Across the border the Tsari, joined by two other Tibetan rivers, the Chayul and the Char, becomes the Subansiri, which flows down through Assam and into the great Brahmaputra. The Tsari itself is both short and high – little more than 40km (24 miles) in length from its source, while its narrow central valley lies at an altitude of approximately 3,500m (almost 11,500ft). The mountain passes on the left hand side of the valley run north back towards Tibet's greatest river the Tsangpo, while those on the right run south to the Indian border. At its eastern end the Tsari makes a clean breach through the southern flank of the Himalaya, which draws in the moisture coming up from the Bay of Bengal. This combination of geography and meteorology makes the Tsari valley, unlike its dry neighbours, wet and lushly vegetated.

In 1913 two Indian Army Captains, Bailey and Moreshead, were the first westerners to visit Tsari. They had entered Tibet from the far north-east of Assam on a secretive journey to survey the eastern section of the India-Tibet frontier, in preparation for the 1914 Simla Tripartite Border Conference. Many years later Bailey was to describe Tsari and its surrounds in his book *No Passport to Tibet*. Unfortunately his personal interests were in fauna rather than flora and his references to plants are rare.

Another 22 years went by before a western botanist reached Tsari when, in 1935, Frank Kingdon Ward entered Tibet from western Assam. Walking east he reached Tsari, stopping there only briefly before proceeding on to his real destination, the Tsangpo Gorge area to the north-east. Nevertheless he made time to find and record a considerable number of plants in Tsari, which he later described in his book *Assam Adventure*. Kingdon Ward passed on advice to the next visitors to Tsari, two more famous plant hunters Frank Ludlow and George Sherriff, who were joined later by (Sir) George Taylor. In 1936 they trekked eastwards into Tibet from Bhutan, equipped to spend a whole year in the Tsari area. It is not surprising

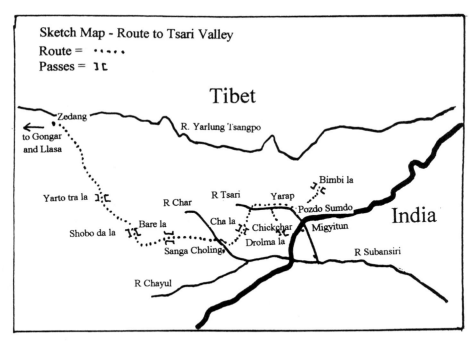

The route of the 1999 expedition to the Tsari Valley

that, in terms of plant discoveries, Tsari is most closely associated with these two. Their experiences in 1936, and also during a second visit in 1938, are described in Dr Harold Fletcher's book, *A Quest of Flowers*, based on the Ludlow and Sherriff journals.

More than 60 years was to elapse before another generation of westerners would be given permission to enter the Tsari valley. The river, as has been described, runs down to the India-Tibet border. The Chinese took control of Tibet in 1950 and have never recognised the 'McMahon Line', the India-Tibet border running along the crest of the Himalayas, agreed between the British and Tibetan Governments under the 1914 Simla Convention. It was this still unresolved issue that more recently provoked the brief Sino-Indian war of 1962.

Unsurprisingly access to this border area by foreigners remains difficult. In 1998 a group organised by the adventure travel specialist Exodus, and led by Kenneth Cox, had their permit to enter the Tsari Valley revoked at the last minute, although they were allowed to explore the far side of some of the passes that lead into the valley from the north. In 1999 our group, again organised by Exodus and led by Kenneth Cox, set off, aware that we too might run into problems on the ground with the Chinese authorities. As it turned out we were fortunate and thanks to good planning achieved all our objectives, with one minor exception.

Travelling from London via Kathmandhu our party of 17 arrived at Llasa

Airport on 8 June. The Airport is at Gongar, some 100km (60 miles) south of Llasa in the Tsangpo valley, and conveniently situated on the road east that all plant-loving visitors to Tibet must travel. Driving on a good tarmac road we soon reached Zedang, Tibet's third largest town. Here we refuelled (there are no petrol stations beyond) and turned south onto a dirt road, to drive into the heart of the Himalaya of SE Tibet. By the end of the second day, and having crossed three high passes of around 5,000m (16,000ft), we reached the Monastery of Sanga Choling. Before its destruction in the Cultural Revolution this was one of the largest Bhuddist Monasteries in Tibet. Still today, in its reconstructed but reduced form, it sits, spectacularly, on an escarpment looking out over the hot dry Char valley. On our return journey we were received courteously by the Monks and shown around. They claimed we were the first western visitors to the Monastery since the 1930s – but if this was really true, the novelty seemed to cause them very little excitement.

That night we camped by a river, among *Primula sikkimensis* and *Iris decora*, at the foot of the Cha La, the last pass we had to cross to reach the Tsari valley. As our vehicles climbed up the north side of the pass the next day, we saw the first rhododendrons. We scrambled up the hillside to find in flower *R. aganniphum*, *R. principis*, *R. primuliflorum* and *R. nivale*. Here also were the almost black flowers of *Thermopsis barbata* and the spectacular slipper orchid *Cypripedium tibeticum*. Later nearing the 5,000m (16,000ft) summit of the Cha la we saw deep purple *Primula*

calderiana, yellow *Fritillaria cirrhosa*, *Primula muscarioides* and the beautiful blue hummock forming *Chionocharis hookeri*. Just below the summit we stopped by a nomadic yak herders' tent, accepting the invitation for some of us to sit with the family by the fire inside and drink salt yak butter tea.

On the southern descent from the pass the near bank of the river was awash with shades of *R. aganniphum* from deep pink in bud to light pink or white in flower (see Fig. 13). Throughout the next 10 days this was to be a constant sight on the hillsides, and the impact of this mass of colour never failed to impress. *R. aganniphum* is so named, incidentally, for the snowy white of the indumentum of its juvenile leaves. I came across a berberis in flower with distinctly blue leaves which I believe was *B. temolaica*, or an affinity. On the far side of the river the hillside was covered with what we agreed was the yellow form of another Taliensia species, *R. phaeochrysum* – but this was a plant we were to see more closely once we had reached Tsari.

By mid afternoon we at last entered the upper end of the Tsari valley, and soon a fine vista opened up of the Senguti plain (see Fig. 14), a broad valley of green water meadows, narrowing in the distance to a gorge as the river approaches the Indian border at its eastern end. To the far right were snow covered mountains around Takpa Shiri 6,000m (19,000ft), not a high peak by Himalayan standards, but one of the most holy for Tibetan Buddhism. Around it two pilgrimages, the Kinkhor, which is annual, and the Ringhkor which occurs every 12th year and takes three months, begin and end in the Tsari valley. Because of this religious connection, the growing of crops and the killing of animals has traditionally been forbidden in the upper part of the valley. This has assisted in the conservation of the valley, which we found to be tranquil and quite unspoilt.

We camped for several nights about halfway down the valley near Yarap, one of the very few small settlements. Here there is the only bridge to the south side of the river, which at this point is about 30m (100ft) in width. Our campsite on the south bank of the river was a yak meadow covered in yellow and purple shades of *Primula alpicola*. Bailey describes camping in this same place in 1913, and on our first morning we followed the route he had taken around the shoulder of the hill south of our meadow and into a small side valley called Chickchar. Here we came to a wayside shrine and then, further up the valley, a small monastery dedicated to Dorji Pharma, the only female incarnation of the Bhudda. It came as a shock to see, even in this remote and barely inhabited place, the ruins of the original monastery close by, destroyed in the 60s by zealots of the Cultural Revolution. Within the Chickchar valley there was much *R. aganniphum* in flower, also the delightful dwarf pink *R. fragariiflorum*, and a deep magenta coloured form of *R. nivale*.

As we reached the southern extremity of the valley we started to climb a steep track up the Drolma La, a pass which leads directly south to the Indian border. With altitude other rhododendron species appeared. First there was *R. wardii*, in its form with a central purple blotch typical of the Ludlow & Sherriff collections. Then there was *R. luciferum,* a species of subsect. Lanata and apparently endemic to this area. *R. luciferum* is so called because the long leaves have a particularly handsome, woolly, chocolate-coloured indumentum which traditionally has been used locally for lamp wicks. This species seems not to have been introduced into cultivation, but could make a good addition as a large garden plant. We saw many ancient stands of *R. luciferum* in dense thickets up to 10m (30ft) tall, here and elsewhere around Tsari, more than 100 perhaps even 200 years old. Unfortunately, by June, they had virtually finished flowering and we saw only one or two of the pale yellow flowers still remaining.

Higher up another rhododendron was in flower. This was the yellow-flowered species of subsect. Taliensia, already mentioned, which Peter and Kenneth Cox have so far classified as *R. phaeochrysum* aff. yellow. This too is a plant not known to be in cultivation (see Fig. 15). Along the trail upwards were many examples of the rhododendron's promiscuous ability to hybridise – *R. luciferum* crossed with *R. aganniphum* and *R. wardii, R. phaeochrysum* crossed with both, and *R. wardii* crossed with *R. aganniphum* – one can never be quite sure. On a cliff face just off the path someone found the beautiful blue *Paraquilegia grandiflora* in flower, and also at ground level at this altitude was the dark blue *Primula tanneri* subsp. *tsariensis*. By mid afternoon we had reached a lake at 4,800m (15,800ft), surrounded by stands of *R. aganniphum*, which marked the beginning of the watershed level of the

. *12:* Rhododendron pudorosum *near the campsite at Yarap in the Tsari valley, SE Tibet (see p.49)*

Fig. 13: Rhododendron aganniphum *on the Cha La, SE Tibet, on the journey to the Tsari valley (see p.47)*

Fig. 14: The view down the Tsari valley, SE Tibet, with the Senguti plain in the foreground (see p.47)

g. 15: Rhododendron phaeochrysum *aff. on the olma La, SE Tibet (see p.48)*

Fig. 16: Camellia *'Loretta Feathers' (see p.40)*

g. 17: Camellia *'Mandalay Queen' (see p.40)*

Fig. 18: Camellia *'Mouchang' (see p.41)*

Fig. 19 (left): the large Pieris forrestii *at Sheringham Park (see p.37) .*
Fig. 20 (below right): Rhododendron *'Brittania' at Sheringham Park (see p.37)*
Fig 21 (bottom): Sheringham Park - the view from the north tower (see p.36)

pass. Some went higher, but I was happy to descend to the Monastery at Chickchar where the Monks invited us in for a very welcome bowl of lemon tea and a rest – it was after all our first days walking at altitude – before strolling the last few miles back to camp as the light faded.

On the following two days some of us explored two other routes leading to the south out of the Tsari valley. The first, called locally the Yarap Cha Na, proved very rewarding. In the first half hour ascending through deciduous woodland from our camp, we came across *R. pudorosum* in flower (see Fig. 12). We had seen this rhododendron, which is a member of subsect. Grandia and rare in cultivation, in profusion above our camp but long since finished flowering. Here under the forest cover two old drawn up trees retained some distinctive pale pink flowers in just about good enough condition to photograph. Higher up the path, in addition to many more variations of natural hybrids (mainly between *R. wardii*, the yellow *R. phaeochrysum* and *R. aganniphum*), there was a particularly good specimen of *R. dignabile*, another member of subsect. Taliensia, with pale yellow flowers. As we approached the watershed of the pass we came onto a shoulder of land forming a great amphitheatre with a lake in the foreground, surrounded by *Primula alpicola* and yellow and bronze *Fritillaria cirrhosa* and with a backdrop of low cliffs. On the cliffs there stood out quite a large area of a deeper red than the now familiar *R. aganniphum*, but too far away to be immediately identifiable. After a scramble up it was found to be a rhododendron new to us,

but one that we had particularly hoped to find – *R. thomsonii* subsp. *lopsangianum*. This is a low growing form of *R. thomsonii*, smaller in all its parts, and another rhododendron probably only to be found within the vicinity of the Tsari valley. This subspecies was discovered by Ludlow & Sherriff in 1936 at the eastern end of the valley and given as its epithet one of the names of the then Dalai Lama. It was exciting to find this most photogenic rhododendron at the peak of its flowering season. There were probably some natural hybrids also among the group. We were not to find this rhododendron anywhere else during our trip. On the way down I saw a single flowering plant of the diminutive *R. pumilum*.

The second, so called, pass some miles to the west of our camp, was, according to our local guide, called Arongajoon dang na, meaning in Tibetan 'the Yak meadow shaped like an 'A' '. We **did indeed** traverse an enormous expanse **of grass** of roughly that shape, studded **with summer** gentians, anemones, pediculars **and** clumps of *R. fragariiflorum*. Thereafter as we climbed higher there were stunning views down to Tsari but disappointment so far as rhododendrons were concerned, for we found nothing new. My finds of the day were restricted to a solitary dwarf *Lilium nanum* in flower, and an attractive shiny leafed but as yet unidentified sorbus.

In the evening, on the way down, I managed to descend the wrong side of a wide stream and found myself ensnared in an extensive forest of ancient *R. aganniphum*. The only sensible way back onto the right path was to crawl on hands and knees downhill under the labyrinthine branches of the *R. aganniphum*, and then wade across the stream

It had been agreed we should spend the second half of our nine-day stay in Tsari descending the valley eastwards to the limit of our permit, and then climbing a pass leading north called the Bimbi La. As we walked down the rough road of the valley we found ourselves amongst much fine blotched *R. wardii* in flower, while by the river bank there were tall trees of *R. luciferum* and other deciduous trees including *Sorbus*, an unknown cherry (not *Prunus serrula*), *Betula* and *Acer*. On the far bank the hillside was covered with untouched forest of *Abies densa*; logging in Tsari appears so far only to be for local needs, and the absence of bridges seems to have protected the south side of the river completely. There were also some good herbaceous plants – the tall yellow-green spring flowering *Gentiana stylophora* (syn. *Megacodon stylophorus*), *Primula involucrata*, *Meconopsis paniculata*, a large-flowered white *Clematis montana* and, perhaps best of all, the only examples of the blue poppy *Meconopsis betonicifolia* that we found in the Valley.

It proved an exciting morning. After a mile or so we came on four or five plants of a rhododendron which Kenneth Cox identified as *R. miniatum*. This is a species related to *R. sherriffii* but never introduced. It was found more or less at the same spot by Ludlow & Sherriff and named for its flame-coloured flowers. It is an early flowerer and we found just one vestigial example that confirmed the colour. The leaves are similar in shape to *R. sherriffii* but the indumentum is whitish. *R. sherriffii* itself was found by Ludlow & Sherriff further south, virtually on the border. These were the only examples of *R. miniatum* we found. Another rarity we found in the same vicinity was a white-flowered poppy *Meconopsis argemonantha*.

By now we had arrived at Pozdo Sumdo, named on the map but otherwise no more than a turning in the track. I was told it means in Tibetan 'the end of Tibet where three rivers join', and our permit did not allow us to go further. In fact the actual border with India is a mile or two further down at Migyitun but there is a Chinese Army base there so we could not afford to take any risks. Instead we turned left and started to climb north up the forest track leading to the Bimbi La. Both Kingdon Ward and Ludlow & Sherriff had also left the valley by this pass.

Almost immediately on this track we came on some mature specimens of *R. fulvum*, not in flower. Close by were many plants of *R. cinnabarinum* var. *purpurellum*, still in flower and worth photographing. A little higher, and among some tall bamboo, came another good find, the bright pink new growth and distinctive bristled stalks of *R. erosum*, one of the most eastern species of subsect. Barbata. Higher still hanging from a rock face to the right of the trail were some large plants of *Paraquilegia grandiflora*, both blue and white flowered.

We camped for a night at 4,000m (12,000ft), in a yak meadow dense with *Primula alpicola*, and continued the climb upwards the following morning through *R. luciferum* forest and around a spectacular waterfall with a drop of at least 300m (1,000ft). For two further nights we made our highest camp of the trip at 4,600m (15,000ft), with magnificent views all round of mountain sides coloured pink and white from the mass of the cover of *R. aganniphum* and looking back down to Tsari and across to the Takpa Shiri mountain complex to the south. Two additional rhododendrons were found in this area – a single plant of *R. calostrotum* and some good plants of *R. laudandum* var. *temoense* in flower, the scaly underside of the leaf almost black. But the main object of the walk to the top of the Bimbi La (4,825m or 15,600ft) and the day spent there, was to explore the many alpines, including *Primula ioessa*, *P. tanneri* subsp. *tsariensis* and *P. dryadiflora*, *Rheum nobile*, *Rhodiola himalensis*, *Androsace delavayi*, *Corydalis*, *Diapensia himalaica* and *Saussurea*.

The descent from the Bimbi La produced one disappointment. By 3,300m (10,000ft) we had reached the area where, according to their 1936 field notes, Ludlow & Sherriff found *R. tsariense*. But not even the eagle-eyed Kenneth Cox could see a trace. Three of us spent some time searching the cliff on the far side of the river through binoculars (it is said to grow on rocky ledges) but could see nothing. We had hoped to camp for our last night at the foot of the Bimbi La, to give ourselves time to search further for *R. tsariense*, but when we reached the road our Tibetan drivers told us that the Chinese Army Commander had come by and ordered us to return further up the valley

to camp. So reluctantly we had to abandon the hunt. It was ironic that after 10 days in Tsari it should be the eponymous *R. tsariense* itself that we failed to find.

We all felt tremendously privileged to have been able to spend a short time in this distant and beautiful place. Two random statistics hint at the richness of the flora of the Tsari valley: (1) the post trip plant list recorded 21 identified species of *Primula*, virtually all in Tsari or its approaches, and (2) two members of our group, specialists in the genus, found no less than 13 species of *Gentiana*. As for rhododendrons, while Tsari does not have the extraordinary diversity to be found on the Doshong La further to the north-east in Tibet, or in areas of the Chinese Provinces of Yunnan or Sichuan, we now know it remains home to at least six unusual and probably endemic species. Tsari is also at something of a rhododendron crossroads. Among the 20 or so species recorded, we saw Chinese taxa all at their western limit, such as *R. fulvum*, *R. wardii* and species of the diverse subsect. Taliensia, alongside Himalayan relatives, species of subsects. Cinnabarina, Lanata, Barbata and Thomsonii, approaching their eastern extremity.

For a rhododendron lover it all made for a fascinating trip, and one long to be remembered.

Philip Evans is a member of the Group and, as Hon. Editor of the Year Book, a member of the Executive Committee. He has made several plant trips to the Sino-Himalaya area

THE GROUP'S PLANT COLLECTIONS

During John Bond's Chairmanship the Group has been responsible for establishing three different collections. The Group's own collection of 'hardy hybrid' rhododendrons being planted at Ramster was the subject of an article in the Year Book 2000. A collection of species rhododendrons has been donated to the RHS as part of the replanting of Battleston Hill at the RHS Garden Wisley, and is now marked there by a plaque. And then in May 2000 Sir Simon Hornby, President of the RHS, opened a collection of Rustica Flore Pleno azaleas planted as a Memorial to Alan Hardy, also on Battleston Hill and again marked with a plaque. Carolyn Hardy and her two daughters, together with the Group's Chairman and members of the Executive Committee attended the opening ceremony.

The Group's Hardy Hybrid Rhododendron Collection at Ramster

Alice Martineau
Antoon Van Welie
Arthur Bedford
Ascot Brilliant
Bagshot Ruby
Baron de Bruin
Beauty of Littleworth
Bernard Crisp
Betty Wormald
Blue Bell
Blue Danube
Blue Peter
Britannia
Butterfly
Caractacus
Caucasicum Pictum
Cetawayo
Chionoides
Christmas Cheer
Constant Nymph
Corry Koster
Countess of Athlone
Countess of Derby
Cunningham's White
Cynthia
David
Diphole Pink
Distinction
Donald Waterer
Doncaster
Dr. A. W. Enditz
Elspeth
Earl of Donoughmore

Everestianum
Faggetter's Favourite
Fastuosum Flore Pleno
Frank Galsworthy
Furnival's Daughter
General Eisenhower
Goldfort
Goldsworth Pink
Goldsworth Yellow
Gomer Waterer
Helen Schiffner
Hollandia
Hon Jean Marie de
    Montague
Hugh Koster
Hyperion
James Burchett
Janet Ward
John Walter
John Waterer
Kate Waterer
Kluis Sensation
Kluis Triumph
Lady Annette de Trafford
Lady Claremont
Lady Clementine
    Mitford
Lady Eleanor Cathcart
Lady Grey Egerton
Lady Longman
Lamplighter
Langworth
Lavender Girl

Lees Dark Purple
Lord Roberts
Louis Pasteur
Madame de Bruin
Marchioness of
    Lansdowne
Marinus Koster
Mars Mount Everest
Michael Waterer
Midsummer
Moser's Maron
Mrs Anthony Waterer
Mrs A. T. de la Mare
Mrs C. B. van Ness
Mrs Charles Pearson
Mrs Davies Evans
Mrs E. C. Sterling
Mrs Furnival
Mrs G. W. Leak
Mrs Helen Koster
Mrs J. C. Williams
Mrs J. G. Millais
Mrs J Waterer
Mrs Lindsay Smith
Mrs Lionel de Rothschild
Mrs P. D. Williams
Mrs Philip Martineau
Mrs R. S. Holford
Mrs Tom Agnew
Mrs Tom Lowinsky
Mrs W.C. Slocock
Mrs W. Watson
Mrs William Agnew

Nimbus
Nobleanum Venustum
Nova Zembla
Old Port Purple
Olga
Peter Koster
Picotee
Pink Pearl
Prince Camille de Rohan
Prof. Hugo de Vries
Prof. J H Zaayer
Purple Splendour
Rainbow
Sappho
Snowflake
Snow Queen
Souvenir de Dr S. Enditz
Souvenir of Anthony
    Waterer
Souvenir of W.C. Slocock
Splendour
Starfish
Susan
Sweet Simplicity
The Bride
Unique
Unknown Warrior
Warrior
White Swan
Wilgens Ruby
Windlesham Scarlet
Windsor Lad

Note. This records the 127 varieties that have been planted (mainly 3 of each) up to and including the autumn of 2000

The Alan Hardy Memorial Collection of Azalea Rustica Flore Pleno

The collection of these unusual double flowered 19th century azaleas, related to the Ghents, and a great favourite of Alan Hardy's, was put together from mainly Belgian sources and over time by Colin Tomain (Starborough Nurseries), a member of the Group and the RHS Rhododendron and Camellia Committee.

Aida	Phebe
Ariadne	Phidias
Corneille	Praxitelle
Fenelon	Quentin Metsys
Freya	Racine
Il Tasso	Raphael de Smet
Mecene	Ribera
Milton	Teniers
Murillo	Velasques
Nora	Virgile
Norma	

The Battleston Hill Rhododendron Species Collection

Rhododendron aberconwayi
Rhododendron aganniphum var. *aganniphum* Doshongense Group
Rhododendron aganniphum var. *flavorufum*
Rhododendron alutaceum
Rhododendron annae
Rhododendron annae Laxiflorum Group
Rhododendron arboreum
Rhododendron arboreum
Rhododendron arboreum subsp. *delavayi*
Rhododendron argyrophyllum subsp. *nankingense* 'Chinese Silver' AGM
Rhododendron balfourianum
Rhododendron barbatum

Rhododendron bhutanense
Rhododendron brachyanthum subsp. *brachyanthum*
Rhododendron brachyanthum subsp. *hypolepidotum*
Rhododendron bureaui AGM
Rhododendron bureauoides
Rhododendron bureauoides
Rhododendron calophytum AGM
Rhododendron calophytum AGM
Rhododendron campanulatum
Rhododendron campylocarpum
Rhododendron campylogynum
Rhododendron concinnum
Rhododendron concinnum
Rhododendron coriaceum
Rhododendron davidsonianum Bodnant Form
Rhododendron decorum
Rhododendron degronianum
Rhododendron dendrocharis
Rhododendron denudatum
Rhododendron edgeworthii AGM
Rhododendron falconeri AGM
Rhododendron floribundum
Rhododendron fortunei 'Sir Charles Butler'
Rhododendron glanduliferum
Rhododendron heliolepis var. *heliolepis*
Rhododendron hodgsonii
Rhododendron huanum
Rhododendron kesangiae EGM 061
Rhododendron lacteum
Rhododendron lanigerum
Rhododendron longipes var. *longipes*
Rhododendron mallotum
Rhododendron neriiflorum
Rhododendron ochraceum
Rhododendron oreotrephes
Rhododendron pachytrichum var. *monosematum*

Rhododendron pachytrichum var.
 monosematum
Rhododendron pachytrichum var.
 pachytrichum 'Sesame'
Rhododendron parmulatum
Rhododendron pocophorum
Rhododendron prattii
Rhododendron pubescens
Rhododendron racemosum
Rhododendron rubiginosum
Rhododendron siderophyllum
Rhododendron sphaeroblastum var.
 wumengense
Rhododendron strigillosum

Rhododendron taliense
Rhododendron taliense
Rhododendron uvariifolium
 'Reginald Childs'
Rhododendron vernicosum
Rhododendron wardii
Rhododendron yunnanense
Rhododendron yunnanense
Rhododendron yunnanense
 'Openwood' AGM
Rhododendron yunnanense
 'Openwood' AGM
Rhododendron zaleucum

THE PHOTOGRAPHIC COMPETITION

There was again a very encouraging number of entries, of both transparencies and prints, for the competition this year from a wide range of the Group membership. Thanks are due in particular to the increasing number of overseas members who have gone to the expense of mailing in entries. The quality was high, and the subject matter throughout varied and interesting which increased the judge's difficulties in selecting the best three. For this reason as happened last year, one or two of the entries that did not make the top three are also printed with acknowledgement.

In third place is Mr John Wilkes-Jones' print entry of a deciduous azalea grown by himself from seed collected at Portmeirion (see Fig. 33). Dr George Hargreaves' beautiful transparency of *Magnolia* 'Mark Jury' (see Fig. 32) is placed second. However the winner of the 2001 competition and the prize of £25 is Mr J C Rees for his transparency of *Rhododendron* 'Cinnkeys' (see Fig. 31), photographed in his own garden in Kent – a hybrid that was raised by E Magor by crossing *R. cinnabarinum* subsp. *cinnabarinum* with *R. keysii*. Congratulations to Mr Rees and the two runners up, and thanks to all the entrants for their efforts and the high standard.

THE MAGNOLIAS OF BAYSWATER

JOEY WARREN

A lady, being driven in London, glanced up a side street and gasped with surprised delight to see an avenue of magnolia trees in full bloom. She noted that they were standard trees, and her question to me was, 'Where can I get a standard magnolia tree like that?'

She was able to identify the street from a map, Sunderland Terrace in Bayswater, London W2, which lies within the City of Westminster (see Fig. 23). The Arboricultural Manager, Paul Akers, said they planted 12 standard *M.* 'Heaven Scent' (*M. liliiflora* × [*M.* × *veitchii*]) in 1992, all of which were about 4m (12ft) tall and containerised stock from Hillier Nurseries of Winchester. Each tree was planted into a newly created tree pit, about 1m (3ft) cube, and filled with new top soil. The trees were watered during the first growing season (1993) and have received general maintenance when necessary since.

There were no failures due to transplantation and no vandalism.

Before this, Sunderland Terrace only had two lime trees, which were outgrowing their situation. This street is in the Westbourne Conservation Area, has east-west orientation and was selected to ascertain if tree planting in its pavements was feasible. The City of Westminster instigated their tree planting programme in 1972, and have planted several thousand new trees of numerous species including *Magnolia* within the eight square miles since then.

Photographs were taken in 1995, and five years on, the magnolia trees have grown well and are a beautiful addition to our urban streets.

Joey Warren is Hon Secretary of the Group and a member of the Executive Committee

GROUP TOUR TO CHESHIRE AND NORTH WALES

COMPILED BY CYNTHIA POSTAN

For our millennium tour on 5-11 May we returned to the North West, not visited since 1984 (*Rhododendrons with Camellias and Magnolias* 1984/85, p.27). For the second year we had no Group Organizer, and the administration and logistics were shared by a team consisting of our Hon. Secretary, Joey Warren, our Hon. Treasurer, Chris Walker, and the Chairman of the North Wales and North West branch, Ken Hulme, who chose the gardens and was our link with the generous owners. We are deeply grateful for their meticulous planning. Special thanks are due to Chris who handled the finances but for business reasons had to leave us before the end. John Bond, our Chairman, who was unavoidably prevented from joining us, was sadly missed. We stayed comfortably, indeed luxuriously, in two hotels: Mollington Banastre, two miles from Chester, and the Royal Celtic Hotel at Caernarfon. These were conveniently placed for our visits for which we had our usual coach and competent driver.

Newton House and Ness

Our first visit on Saturday was to Newton House owned by Mr and Mrs D Harsant, members of the North Wales branch, who have a 0.3ha (¾ acre) garden planted over the last 30 years. Lawns with hedge-backed borders and island beds planted with species and hybrid rhododendrons surround the house. In one corner are hybrids from the American Pacific Northwest including R. 'Halfdan Lem', R. 'Lem's Cameo' and R. 'Odee Wright'. Further along is a wonderful plant of the R. *haematodes* hybrid 'W.F.H.' with its rich dark red flowers. In the prolific kitchen garden are R. 'Fragrantissimum', R. *decorum* and R. *edgeworthii*, while others of the Maddenia subsection are in pots. The summer house is surrounded by hybrids R. 'Crest', R. Romany Chai Group and R. *davidsonianum*. Here Mrs Harsant was presented with R. *wasonii* by David Farnes.

Nearby, also in Heswall, is Brackenbank, home of Mrs H B Chrimes and her late husband, Chancellor of Liverpool University. The house, on a sandstone promontory, overlooks a natural valley replanted in 1962. The first impression from above is of a sea of colour, with the taller R. 'Loderi Venus', R. *augustinii* and R. *orbiculare* most obvious. Walking down into the valley, we looked at R. 'Lady Chamberlain', R. 'Lady Rosebery', R. 'Winsome', R. 'Psyche', R. 'Fabia' and splashes of red from *R.* 'W.F.H.' and *R.* 'May Day'. Also in the valley among birch and sorbus is a tall *Magnolia* 'Heaven Scent', presented to Mrs Chrimes by our Group during our 1984 visit. On the far side of the valley, through the perfume of deciduous azaleas, we looked up into a group of Corsican pines (*Pinus nigra* subsp. *laricio*) growing on the sandstone cliff in a dramatic setting. Ken Hulme gave Mrs Chrimes an azalea 'Anneka', along with our grateful thanks.

Lunch was at the Boathouse at Parkgate overlooking the Dee. The river has long since silted up and Chester is no longer the thriving medieval port it once was. The afternoon was spent at Ness Botanic Gardens where Ken Hulme was Director for 32 years. We were fortunate in having him as our guide. A K Bulley began gardening here in 1898 and sponsored, among others, the plant collectors George Forrest, Frank Kingdon Ward and R E Cooper. The estate was given to the University of Liverpool in 1948 by Bulley's daughter.

At the Education Centre we saw the impressive Rhododendron Show of the North West and North Wales Branch of which Ken is Chairman. Ken began his tour by telling us how some of the hard landscaping in the garden had been acquired. Paving included railway slabs and Quaker gravestones and the slates on the roof of the visitor centre had come from the old village school.

At the main rhododendron border we were joined by Dr Hugh McAllister, who showed us the results of his crosses of subsection Saluenense which he wrote about

in his article 'Chromosome numbers in Rhododendrons' (*Rhododendrons with Camellias and Magnolias 1993*, p. 24). Some of the rhododendrons in this border showed drought stress. Walking through the cooler woodland behind we saw *R. macabeanum* grafted from the Trewithen plant, said to be the finest yellow-flowering rhododendron in the western world. Ken told us a cautionary tale about the nectar of *R. cinnabarinum* and *R. luteum* which can knock you out if you lick it, and we learnt also that *R. yunnanense* and *R. decorum* are drought tolerant but need moisture in May and June when the young shoots appear. Dr McAllister advised us against too much mulch. The roots of rhododendrons need air and mulch keeps moisture out.

Elsewhere we saw a lovely magnolia, *M. acuminata* var. *subcordata* 'Miss Honeybee' and wonderful plantings of deciduous azaleas. We walked on through areas providing year-round interest, including heathers, alpine plants, a rock garden and a bog garden, until we came to the terraces built from the discarded Walton-on-the-Hill railway station; another example of Ken's recycling activities while he was director. Joey Warren thanked Ken and Hugh for a memorable visit. That evening Ken gave us a most valuable talk, with illustrations, on how to identify the various members of the Maddenia subsection which will help us all in the future.

Jo White

Arley Hall

We set off early on Sunday to visit Arley Hall where Lord and Lady Ashbrook first showed us their own private garden, The Old Parsonage, delightfully laid out with borders and lawns sweeping down to a pond surrounded by bog-loving plants and rhododendrons, azaleas and interesting trees. *Exochorda × macrantha* 'The Bride' was a snowy mound of white flowers and *Halesia monticola* var. *vestita*, the snowdrop tree, was in full flower and scented. Nearby was a fabulous *R*. 'Loderi Venus', pale pink, blowsy and so sweetly scented. Other hybrids included *R*. 'Ightham Yellow' (*R. wardii × R. decorum*), a magnificent specimen, and *R*. 'The Master' (*R*. 'Humming Bird' × *R. griersonianum*) with rose pink flowers. A striking combination was *R*. 'Winsome', red in bud but opening paler, and *R*. 'Susan' (*R. campanulatum × R. fortunei*), lavender. In the bog garden *Darmera peltatum* was pushing up its tall flowers. Hostas, ferns, irises and large stands of *Gunnera manicata* promised summer interest. Unusual trees were *Aesculus parviflora*, its gorgeous flowers just appearing, *Taxus* 'Dovastonia' and a lovely weeping *Rubus tridel* with striking white flowers. *Magnolia* 'Heaven Scent' was also in flower.

We then walked to the Grove, a rhododendron woodland, planted by Lord Ashbrook 25 years ago. An unfavourable site at first glance as the soil is clay. Wet boggy conditions lead to solid dry caked soil in summer: a problem, but the soil is acid and in late years the Cheshire County Council have supplied leaf sweepings which, combined with bark chippings, has proved effective. Filtered shade has allowed rhododendrons, magnolias and camellias to thrive. *C*. 'Elsie Jury' is impressive.

Rhododendron hybrids seen were 'Naomi' 'Virginia Richards', 'Unique' with brigh pink buds opening to cream flowers, 'Pin Gin' (*R. yunnanense* × 'Lady Rosebery') light solferino purple shading to peach and 'Blueberry', a *R. roxieanum* hybrid Smaller rhododendrons included *R rigidum album, R. hippophaeoides, R.* 'Con tina' (*R. concinnum × R. augustinii*) wit vivid violet blue flowers, *R*. 'Anna Bald siefen' with clear phlox pink flowers wit deeper margins and *R*. 'Emasculum' (*R. cil iatum × R. dauricum*) which looks unusua without stamens. 'Chinese Silver' (AM 1957) is the finest form of *R. argyrophyl lum* subsp. *nankingense* with attractiv frilly flowers and silver indumentum. Bot *Magnolia soulangeana* 'Lennei' with dar purple pink flowers and *Cornus nuttalli* were looking magnificent.

We walked to the main gardens alon; the terrace where *R*. 'Mrs A.T. de la Mare (white) and *R*. 'Susan' (lavender) made pretty combination. In the garden prope the herbaceous borders (planted in 1846 with the buttress hedges (added in 1870 were beginning to show their wonderfu variations in greenery. To the left the ile columns, standing like a row of sentinels confuse many visitors. They are not hollie as people suppose, but holm oaks (*Quercu ilex*). Planted before the war as conica shrubs, they acquired a cylindrical shap after years without care or clipping. The nearly died in 1981 after a severe frost, bu Ken Hulme's advice was to leave wel alone. They slowly recovered and today se off the long lawn leading to the steps an stone vases and frame the distant parklan beyond. Paul Cook (head gardener) an

Tommy Acton (retired head gardener) were most helpful in answering our many questions.

Cholmondeley Castle

In the afternoon we drove to Cholmondeley Castle, built by the Marquess of Cholmondeley between 1801 and 1804 when the cedar of Lebanon (*Cedrus libani*) below the castle was planted. Entering by the Temple Garden with its lake and two grassy islands where rustic bridges lead back to the lake, we saw a magnificent *Cornus nuttallii* 'Portlemouth'. An *Arbutus × andrachnoides* with its cinnamon red bark also caught the eye. The view up to the castle was eclipsed by a wonderful *R. augustinii* and, nearby, *R.* 'Yellow Petticoats' (similar to 'Hotei'). On Tower Hill we saw a healthy *R.* 'Elizabeth' – a cultivar often prone to powdery mildew – while the glades of bluebells surrounded by the yellow, scented *R. luteum* were greatly admired by our overseas friends. The woodland conditions on the hill are ideal for rhododendrons and azaleas: *R.* 'May Day' was flowering well.

Discussions within the group were lively as we had already seen 'May Day' at Brackenbank and 'W.F.H.' at Ness and were keen to identify the difference between the two. 'May Day' (*R. haematodes × R. griersonianum*) has a large frilled calyx, whereas 'W.F.H.' (*R. haematodes ×* 'Tally Ho' [*R. griersonianum × R. facetum*]) has a minute barely visible calyx. Both have tan indumentum from *R. haematodes* and bright red flowers. 'W.F.H.' is named after W F Hamilton, head gardener at Pylewell Park. Back on the terrace by the castle Lady

Cholmondeley showed us the *Ceanothus arboreus* 'Trewithen Blue' which flowers three times a year, and, against the castle walls, two large *Magnolia grandiflora* 'Exbury' and 'Goliath'. We thanked Lady Cholmondeley and presented her with *R. roxieanum*.

Bolesworth Castle

Our third garden was Bolesworth Castle where we were welcomed by Mr and Mrs Anthony Barbour. The Castle was built in the 1820s by George Walmsley, and remodelled in the 1920s by Clough Williams Ellis who designed the Italianate steps and terracing. The gardens were improved in 1988 by Dame Sylvia Crowe, who simplified the layout for ease of maintenance. There are marvellous views over the Cheshire Plain to the Welsh hills. Behind the Castle a wooden bridge leads to a woodland walk which was planted five years ago with trees, rhododendrons, azaleas and camellias. Existing *R. ponticum* was used for wind protection. The list of interesting hybrids and notable specimens is a long one and includes *R. rex* subsp. *fictolacteum*, *R. cinnabarinum* 'Conroy', *R.* 'Viscy' (strange orange and yellow flowers with dark spotting), *R.* 'Queen Elizabeth II' (chartreuse green), *R.* 'Maharini' (creamy yellow), *R.* 'Halfdan Lem', *R.* 'Loderi King George', *R.* 'Naomi', *R.* 'Horizon Monarch' (greenish yellow with red flare) and *R.* 'Arctic Tern' (Peter Cox's *R. ledum* hybrid). Other striking shrubs were a double white *Camellia × williamsii* 'E.T.R. Carlyon', *Cornus* 'Eddie's White Wonder', *Acer rufinerve* 'Albolineatum' (variegated leaves), *Fothergilla major*

Monticola Group, *Cladrastis lutea* (yellow wood) and *Abies concolor* (slate blue needles). A young garden which should mature into an interesting collection. We were grateful for the opportunity to see it.

Morna Knottenbelt

That evening Dr Brenda MacLean who is researching a biography of George Forrest (which has, surprisingly, never yet been attempted) entertained us with the first fruits of her researches. She showed us photographs of Forrest's family as well as his expeditions and told us enough about this heroic character's life to make us eager to read her forthcoming book.

Aberconwy Nursery
Monday was another glorious day and our first visit was to Aberconwy Nursery, Colwyn Bay, owned and impressively run by Dr Keith Lever (a mycologist) and his wife Rachel (a biochemist). They specialize in alpine plants and hellebores, but small rhododendrons are also represented. Rachel is involved in producing F1 hellebores – *H.* × *ballardiae* (*H. niger* × *H. lividus*) and *H.* × *ericsmithii* (*H. niger* × *H. sternii*) and *H. nigercors* (*H. niger* × *H. corsicus*) all of which inherit good marked leaf form and attractive multiple flower heads with colours ranging from heavily flushed red to white or green.

Keith has substantial collections of gentians and primulas and has produced his own gentian hybrids of which the autumn-flowered *Gentiana* 'Shot Silk' (FCC 1992) and a new hybrid *G.* ' Silken Skies' ('Shot Silk' × *G. farreri*) were noted. With primulas he pursues a rigorous hand

pollination routine, crossing thrum- and pin-eyed to maintain true stocks. Not yet in his list *Primula watsonii* (ex ACE 1402) (deep plum *P. muscarioides*) was much admired. One looks forward to seeing it in his very comprehensive list. The Levers showed us round their own garden which was full of lovely plants.

Bodnant
Bright sunshine continued at Bodnant where Martin Puddle kindly escorted us round. The quantity of flowers to be seen passed all expectations, with the famous Bodnant hybrids *R.* 'Matador' (red), *R.* 'Winsome', *R.* 'Vanessa' and *R.* 'Fabia' being particularly impressive. *R. augustinii* and *R. davidsonianum* were also in bloom. However it was the sight of the Dell in full flower, with the Kurume azaleas stealing the show, that was my main memory. Quieter, but just as impressive, were *R. bullatum* and the *R. maddenii* and *R. edgeworthii* hybrids at their peak on the terraces. Gloriously scented, they were a delicious experience.

After thanking Martin Puddle we took leave of Bodnant and journeyed on across Snowdonia to our second hotel, the Royal Celtic at Caernarfon.

Carol Rowe

Bod Hyfryd
Still blessed with fine weather on Tuesday, our coach took us to a remarkable alpine garden, Bod Hyfryd, Penmaenmawr, situated high on the mountainside facing north, overlooking the sea towards Anglesey. Here we were greeted by Dr Good, a biologist by profession, who told

how he had transformed the garden over the past nine years from a total infestation of Japanese knotweed to a paradise of little alpine treasures. We immediately noted how successfully he was growing lewisias not on their sides but placed on top of the wall in the centre of small rocks from the quarry. (The circular centres had been removed and exported as stones in the game of ice curling.) Many interesting alpines were growing in carefully constructed double walls. Familiar to members of our group were the rhododendrons – *R. edgeworthii*, the very prostrate *R. keiskii* 'Yaku Fairy' and the lovely scented *R. primuliflorum*. Other plants which attracted attention were the very floriferous *Paeonia cambessedesii*, the spreading *Pinus mugo*, *Sophora microphylla*, *Azara microphylla*, *Linum arboreum* and a good clump of *Myosotidium hortensia*.

Plas Newydd

We arrived at Plas Newydd in time for a quick lunch before the group divided, some to see the house with its intriguing Rex Whistler mural, the others to walk round the informal garden overlooking the Menai Straits and the vast panorama of Snowdonia. Sadly, a heat haze obliterated the spectacular view. There were fine trees flourishing here. *Acer pseudoplatanus* 'Brilliantissimum', *Eucryphia × intermedia*, *Magnolia sargentiana* var. *robusta*, *Magnolia grandiflora* 'Goliath' and fine specimens of *Embothrium coccineum*. All however, agreed that the highlight of this visit was when the Marquess of Anglesey joined us in the rhododendron wood. Here he made us welcome and explained how in 1947 the

planting had been a wedding present from Lord Aberconway: a lorry load of rhododendrons from Bodnant and two men to plant them – a procedure to be repeated over the next two years. We were all overwhelmed by the results of this generous present which has developed into an outstanding rhododendron woodland garden. The air was scented with glorious maddenia, including *R. lindleyi* and *R. edgeworthii* hybrids. There were some great specimens of *R. macabeanum*, *R. fulvum*, *R.* 'Matador', also a lovely *R.* 'Shilsoni', *R. thomsonii* and *R. fortunei* to mention just a few of the treasures that abound here, all of which seem thoroughly to approve of their habitat. They scatter their fledgelings liberally and the Marquess invited us to help ourselves. So with penknives and bare hands and the help of the coach driver we acquired many new seedlings. The Marquess's enthusiasm infected us all and we enjoyed identifying and discussing the plants. We shall take home many memories of this garden and its generous owner, as well as lasting souvenirs. The woodland also contained fine large magnolias, a white form of *M. sargentii* var. *robusta*, two *M. campbellii*, two *M. × veitchii* and a magnificent *Drimys winteri*. We returned to Caernarfon exhausted but happy.

Nesta Frazer

Crûg Farm

Our final day, Wednesday, of this splendid tour started with a visit to a fascinating nursery and garden at Crûg Farm near Caernarfon owned by Glendwyn and Sue Wynn-Jones. Glendwyn had been a beef farmer but when faced with a £30,000 bill for a slurry tank or £3,000 for a polythene tunnel, the latter option seemed more attractive to the keen gardener. So, in 1990 they started their nursery, working in it three days a week and farming on the other four days until 1992, when they let the farm.

Glendwyn spends about six months each year, mostly in the Far East, collecting plants and seed and now has an amazing collection of rare and unusual shade-tolerant plants in his display garden and upwards of 2,000 species and cultivars in the nursery. Truly a fantastic achievement in the space of a decade.

Portmeirion

We then drove through the mountains to Portmeirion, where we were met by Philip Brown who has been in charge of the gardens since 1981. Philip escorted us by way of the Italianate village of Gothic, Renaissance and Victorian-style buildings enlivened with the scent of *Rhododendron* 'Fragrantissimum', *R.* 'Suave' and their parent *R. edgeworthii* to the subtropical woodland garden covering 70 acres and containing many fine rhododendron specimens, including some gigantic

hybrids of *R. arboreum, R. griersonianum* and *R. fortunei*. Among many outstanding plants were the largest shrubs of *Enkianthus campanulatus, Drimys winteri* and *Viburnum rhytidophyllum* to be seen, probably, anywhere. The sight of a dozen or so of the golden *Rhododendron* 'Saffron Queen' clinging to a steep hillside was quite breathtaking.

Daphne Weston

After one more night in Caernarfon the coach returned us to Chester where the group parted company for their homeward journey. The five days of the tour were spent in perfect weather and all agreed that the choice of gardens and diversity of plants would be hard to equal.

Acknowledgements

The Editor would like to acknowledge the authorship of the individual reports by tour participants Jo White, Morna Knottenbelt, Carol Rowe, Nesta Frazer and Daphne Weston.

Cynthia Postan is a former editor of the Year Book and of the 1996 publication, The Rhododendron Story

DAVID TREHANE

David Cowl Trehane was born on 10 October 1908 in Dorset and died on 4 April 2000 in Cornwall. He graduated in Horticulture from Reading University, and spent his working life in horticulture and local affairs in Dorset, before retiring in 1969 to Trehane, the property he had acquired in Cornwall some years earlier. Here he transformed the six-acre garden from a wilderness into one of the best and most loved in Cornwall, famed for its collections of rhododendrons and camellias, as well as magnolias (including one of the best *M. campbellii*'s in the country which was blown down six years ago but still flowers in a horizontal position). He also had one of the best collections of *Eucryphia* in the country. An article on the garden at Trehane appeared in the February 2000 edition of the RHS Journal, *The Garden*.

David Trehane served as a Director and Vice President of the International Camellia Society, and was a member of the RHS Rhododendron and Camellia Committee. In 1986 he was honoured with the Gold Veitch Memorial Medal of the RHS 'for his contribution to the knowledge and cultivation of camellias and blueberries'. He was also President of the Cornish Garden Society for several years.

'Mr Camellia UK' has, for very many years now, been a title synonymous with the name of David Trehane. It was he who widened the perspective of camellias in this country so that we all became aware that there were camellias other than 'Lady Clare', 'Adolphe Audusson' and 'Gloire de Nantes'. With his wide knowledge and great personal charm he introduced many gardeners to the desirability of the *Camellia* as a genus.

We will always remember his return from the US with slides of the newer American hybrids. With his contacts there and in New Zealand, with people like Dave Feathers and Les and Felix Jury, he introduced many very desirable plants.

David was for many years on the Rhododendron and Camellia Committee of the RHS and with his gold-medal winning exhibits at flower shows did much to popularise the camellia. He was an enormous help to many and very generous with both his knowledge and his plants. When the gardens at Mount Edgecumbe were being rejuvenated he donated many large plants.

In Cornwall he was the backbone of the annual Cornwall Garden Society show in Truro and later in St Austell, and not only for camellias but also for magnolias and other genera in which his knowledge and interest extended.

His garden at Trehane, Probus, Cornwall, was exemplary in many ways and his underplanting was noteworthy. He was especially known as well for growing a wide range of blueberries and at his recommendation I remember growing the inappropriately named 'Bert', which has a wonderful muscat flavour.

David will be very much missed for his knowledge, for his helpful advice and for his personal charm.

Jimmy Smart

Tom Savige

Latterly Patron of the International Camellia Society, Tom Savige died on 19 December 1999 aged 86. He was born at the Northern Rivers locality of Bonalbo in New South Wales, Australia, where his father was a cattle grazier and cedar spotter. After secondary school Tom attended the Royal Melbourne Institute of Technology where he obtained his diploma in Mechanical and Electrical Engineering. He travelled to England and was employed at the Westlands Aircraft Company before returning to Australia on the outbreak of the Second World War, and was then employed at the Commonwealth Aircraft Corporation. He married Olive Steele in 1941, and gardening became part of their way of life.

At the end of the war Tom joined Trans Australia Airlines and became their Technical Representative. He was sent to San Diego in the United States to supervise the purchase of five new aircraft, and was away for over two years. It was during that time in San Diego that he became aware of the immense variety and beauty of camellias which resulted in his lifelong passion, a passion fortunately shared by his wife.

The Saviges joined the newly formed Australian Camellia Research Society. Research was indeed needed to sort out the confusing nomenclature of the genus. In 1920, following a change of job, the Saviges acquired a house in Albury on two

acres of land. One van of household items duly arrived plus two truckloads of camellias. I heard that this eccentric gardener was planting a row of the then rare reticulata camellias. I had just purchased my first, so I determined to meet him.

Tom soon became President of the Albury Horticultural Society and the first President of the Hume branch of the Australian Camellia Research Society. His garden was heavily planted, camellias predominating, but with a collection also of magnolias, azaleas, old world roses and bulbous plants, the whole blending with Australian natives.

The hybrid camellias that Tom produced from the small-flowered species were his greatest achievement, and about 10 of these have been registered, as well as some japonica cultivars. Tom did not spend all his time in the garden. He travelled, and corresponded with camellia enthusiasts worldwide. He had a particular interest in nomenclature and this culminated in the publication in 1993 of *The International Camellia Register*, two large volumes listing 267 camellia species and a mind boggling 32,000 cultivars, all described and cross referenced. A supplement of 390 pages has now been published, for which Tom studied Chinese and Kanji characters in order to translate the names of oriental camellias.

He became President of the International Camellia Society in 1977 and was awarded the Order of Australia Medal for services to horticulture in 1987. In 1992 he was awarded the Gold Veitch Memorial Medal of the RHS, and in 1994 the degree of Master of Science (Agriculture) (*Honoris causa*) by the University of Sydney for his work on *The International Camellia Register*. He also received honours from most of the world's camellia societies.

The Japanese name of the camellia cultivar 'Isaribi' means 'the fire in the prow of night fishing boat to attract fish'. Tom Savige was *isaribi* – he attracted plant lovers to him by his warmth, humour, profound knowledge and enthusiasm, wherever he went.

Ross Hayter

EARLY RHODODENDRON COMPETITION

DAVID FARNES

Although the support for the Early Rhododendron Competition on 14-15 March 2000 was disappointingly low, with only half the number of entries compared with the same competition last year, it is very pleasing to report the most welcome return to the show bench, after a lapse of 75 years, of entries from Tregothnan garden near Truro and the Hon Evelyn Boscawen, who has taken over the property from his parents, Lord and Lady Falmouth. The show also saw the first competition for The Alan Hardy Challenge Salver presented by the Rhododendron, Camellia and Magnolia Group. The trophy is a silver salver, suitably engraved and was won by Edmund de Rothschild and Exbury Garden with a points total of double the number of that of his nearest rival. As in 1999 Vireya rhododendrons dominated the classes for plants grown under glass to the almost total exclusion of anything from section Maddenia – surely a case can be made now for a separate or additional class for these increasingly popular rhododendrons.

Class 1 for three species, one truss of each, was won by the Hon Evelyn Boscawen with *R. macabeanum, R. calophytum* and *R. barbatum*. Second prize to Edmund de Rothschild and Exbury for *R. macabeanum, R. calophytum and R. irroratum* with no other entries in this class.

Class 2 for a spray of a species, was won by Exbury with a magnificent spray of *R. fulvum* (see Fig. 26) bearing 19 trusses all within the exhibit size limitation of the show schedule. Second prize was awarded to the Hon Evelyn Boscawen and Tregothnan with *R. arboreum* var. *roseum* and Major T Spring-Smyth was third with his *R. spinuliferum*.

Class 3 for one truss of a species, had five entries with all the prizes being awarded to the subsect. Grandia. First was awarded to a superb truss of *R. macabeanum* from Tregothnan, second prize to Major T Spring-Smyth for *R. montroseanum* with third going to Brian Wright with his *R. macabeanum*. In such company the two fine trusses of *R. barbatum* had no chance of an award.

Class 4 for one truss of a species in subsects. Arborea or Argyrophylla, was won by Exbury with *R. arboreum* 'Blush'. Second went to A Simons for his *R. hunnewellianum* with third prize to Tregothnan for a blood red *R. arboreum*.

Class 5 for a truss of a species from subsects. Barbata, Glischra or Maculifera, received four entries but only two prizes awarded. First went to Tregothnan with *R. barbatum* and second prize to Exbury also with *R. barbatum*; just reward for their eclipse in Class 3.

Class 6 for a truss of a species in sub-sects. Falconera or Grandia had three entries, all of *R. macabeanum* with Tre-gothnan gaining first prize, Brian Wright second and third going to Exbury.

Classes 7 and 8 had but one entry in each, both from Exbury who was awarded first prize for *R. calophytum* in subsect. For-tunea and first in subsect. Neriiflora for *R. beaneanum*.

Class 9 received no entries.

Class 10 for a spray from a host of 16 subsects., received only three entries with Brian Wright winning with *R. lutescens* (subsect. Triflora). Second prize went to Exbury for *R. racemosum* 'Rock Rose'.

Classes 11 and 12 received no entries, yet in the previous year there were 11 entries alone in Class 11 for a truss of any other species.

Class 13 for one truss each of three hybrids had but one entry; this from Exbury showing 'Nimrod', 'Our Kate' and 'Red Argenteum' for the first prize.

Class 14 for a spray of any hybrid, had again only one entry also from Exbury who gained first prize with 'Lucy Lou'.

Class 15 for one truss of any hybrid was won by N Cassleton Elliott with an Exbury seedling, a lovely truss with superb large flowers. Second prize went to Exbury for their 'Avalanche' and third to Tregoth-nan for a nicely displayed 'Lady Alice Fitzwilliam'.

Class 16 for a truss of a hybrid in which one parent must be a species from a list specified in the Show Schedule, was won, as last year, by Exbury with 'Werei' and second to Tregothnan with an unnamed truss.

Class 17 for a truss of a hybrid in which one parent must be a Fortunea species was won by Exbury with 'Avalanche' with second prize going to N Cassleton Elliott for another truss of his unnamed Exbury seedling. This was a reversal of the prize order in Class 15.

Class 18 for a hybrid of restricted parentage, one truss, was won by Exbury with 'Christmas Cheer' as the only entry.

Class 19 for any other hybrid, received no entries.

Class 20 for a spray of any hybrid not catered for in the foregoing classes was won by Exbury with 'Christmas Cheer', also as the only entry.

Class 21 for a truss of any tender species of hybrid was dominated by entries from section Vireya and five of the six entries gained awards. First prize for 'Shan-tung Rose' was awarded to C Fairweather who also won second prize with 'Toff'. Third prize went to Dr Robbie Jack for his *R. ciliicalyx* – the sole representative of sub-sect. Maddenia in this class. Fourth prize was awarded to A Simons for 'RA' and highly commended to C Fairweather for 'Princess Alexandra', another of his vireyas.

Class 22 for a spray of any tender species or hybrid, had but one entry from C Fairweather who was awarded first prize for a delightful and colourful 'Flamenco Dancer'.

David Farnes

Main Rhododendron Competition ~ Species

Archie Skinner

It is with sadness that I report this competition (25 and 26 April 2000), finding it difficult to be enthusiastic because there was such poor support from so few rhododendron growers – only four. But a big thank you to them for keeping the flag flying, on what we all hope is not a sinking ship.

This is the third year that the rhododendron numbers have been down, unlike the camellia competitions which have been such a success. Overall I felt the hybrids were slightly better quality than the species but nevertheless there were some fine sprays and trusses which gave pleasure and interest.

Class 1, six species, one of each. Exbury Gardens with the only entry became the worthy winners of The Lionel de Rothschild Challenge Cup with *R. metternichii, R. coriacium, R. hypenanthum*, a superb *R. niveum, R. arboreum* 'Rubiayat' and a very pale coloured *R. campanulatum*.

Class 2, three species, one truss of each. *R. orbiculare* (not quite out), *R. irroratum* 'Polka Dot' and *R. crinigerum* won for Exbury.

Class 3, any species, one truss. The McLaren Challenge Cup was awarded to Dr Robbie Jack with *R. pachysanthum* (see Fig. 27) from his garden in Scotland. Second went to Exbury with *R. crinigerum* who also gained third prize with *R. edgeworthii* which although grown outside, was in very good shape.

Class 4, any species, one spray. The only entry, and winner of the Roza Stevenson Challenge Cup was Exbury with a superb, well-staged vase of *R. augustinii*.

Class 5, any species of subsect. Arborea or subsect. Argyrophylla, one truss. First Exbury with a near perfect *R. niveum*. Second Brian Wright with very trim, clean *R. arboreum*.

Class 6, any species of subsect. Barbata, subsect. Glischra or subsect. Maculifera, one truss. Dr Jack's near perfect *R. pachysanthum* beat Exbury's *R. crinigerum* to first prize.

Class 7, any species of subsect. Campanulata, subsect. Fulgensia or subsect. Lanata, one truss. The only entry was from Exbury with a very good *R. campanulatum* (see Fig. 25), very worthy of its first prize.

Class 8, any species of subsect. Grandia or subsect. Falconera, one truss. First prize went to the only entry from Exbury with *R. fictolacteum*.

Class 9, any species of subsect. Fortunea, one truss. Exbury gained a second with *R. orbiculare* which was not quite out.

Class 10, any species of subsect. Fulva, subsect. Irrorata or subsect. Parishia, one truss. First prize went to a very good *R. irroratum* 'Polka Dot' from Exbury.

Class 11, any species of subsect. Taliensia, one truss. A good *R. roxieanum* var. *oreonastes* from Brian Wright gained first prize, closely followed by Dr Jack's *R. agan-niphum* and third prize to Exbury's *R. trail-lianum* var. *dictyotum* 'Kathmandu'.

Class 13, any species of subsect. Pontica, one truss. A very good truss of *R. met-ternichii* from Exbury just beat a *R. degro-nianum* from Dr Jack. It was a very close contest.

Class 14, any species of subsect. Thomsonia, subsect. Selensia or subsect. Campylocarpa, one spray. Exbury gained third prize with *R. wardii* var. *wardii*.

Class 18, any species of subsect. Edgeworthia or subsect. Maddenia, one spray. Exbury was the only entry and gained first prize with *R. johnstonianum*.

Class 19, any species of subsect. Maddenia, one truss. *R. johnstoneanum* from Exbury received first prize.

Class 20, any species of subsect. Triflora and subsect. Heliolepida other than *R. augustinii*, one spray. Exbury's *R. david-sonianum*, a clear bright pink, gained the first and only prize.

Class 21, *R. augustinii,* one spray. A superb vase from Exbury gained first place, just beating a very good vase from A W Simons who was fresh from his success at the camellia competitions. Brian Wright came third.

Class 22, any species of subsect. Cinnabarina, subsect. Tephropepla or sub-sect. Virgata, one spray. The only entry gained first prize for Exbury with *R. cinnabarinum.*

Class 23, any species of subsect. Campylogyna, subsect. Genestieriana or subsect. Glauca, one spray. The single entry from Exbury of *R. glaucophyllum* was awarded first prize.

Class 24, any species of subsect. Lapponica, one spray. A very dark *R. russatum* from Dr Jack gained first, and his *R. hip-pophaeoides* third prize. Exbury came second with *R. scintillans.*

Class 26, species of subsect. Scabrifo-lia, one spray. The only entry, Exbury's *R. spinuliferum,* was awarded first prize.

Class 29, one species of sect. Vireya, one truss grown under glass. A charming *R. macgregoriae* staged by A W Simons gained a well-deserved first prize.

Class 30, any species of deciduous azalea, one spray. First prize went to a vase of *R. dilatatum* from Exbury.

Archie Skinner

MAIN RHODODENDRON COMPETITION ~ HYBRIDS

BRIAN WRIGHT

With only four exhibitors taking part, the 25-26 April 2000 competition was probably the worst supported event in the whole history of the Main Rhododendron Competition and, as such, should be a matter for grave concern.

As a competition it was no contest with Exbury entering 48 of the 58 classes and being awarded 28 first prizes and 24 second and third prizes. It was plainly a David versus Goliath encounter but this time with David coming off very much the worse.

But all credit must go to Exbury, not simply because of their overwhelming success in competition terms but also for their enthusiasm and skill in putting on a show – the competition is, after all, a show of rhododendrons as well as a contest and without Exbury the show would not have gone on in this millennium year.

In the hybrid section, Exbury, as to be expected, had even greater success than in the species section. Of the 22 classes they entered they won 15 first prizes. Among them, the highlights for me were the following.

Class 33, three trusses. Here Exbury showed their own cross, 'Queen of Hearts', a dusky monarch of a plant with black

spotted, dark crimson flowers and dark green foliage, 'Mariloo', again their own cross and one of the great *R. lacteum* hybrids named after Mrs Lionel de Rothschild, and an outstanding 'Loderi Venus', extravagantly impressive on the bush but hardly easy to display on the showbench.

Class 34, any single truss for the Loder Challenge Cup. Sadly this class was a prime example of how poorly the Main Competition was supported. Traditionally, it is the most popular class in the event attracting many entries. On this occasion, however, it displayed only three exhibits, all from Exbury. They were 'Kiev', 'Loderi Venus' and 'Fortune'. Each of which was good enough to take the cup although the judges' decision went to 'Kiev', that splendidly waxy red which Lionel de Rothschild derived from *R. elliottii* and 'Barclayi Robert Fox'.

Class 35, any single spray. This class was won by the popular American hybrid 'Dora Amateis', a white-flowered, highly floriferous, bouquet-like exhibit that was probably the most attractive spray in the competition.

Class 36, three trusses of plants bred and raised in the garden of the exhibitor. With The Crosfield Challenge Cup at stake, Exbury's winning entry here comprised 'Doug Betteridge', 'Gaul' and 'Lionel's Triumph'. Although the ruby red 'Gaul' and the creamy pink 'Lionel's Triumph' are both excellent hybrids, the star of this trio was 'Doug Bettridge'. Doug is Exbury's former head gardener of many years service and a stalwart supporter of the Vincent Square rhododendron competitions. It was therefore cheering to see this fine *R. fortunei* cross with its typical Exbury complexion, creamy lilac-pink flowers, named after him.

Class 44 for *R. griersonianum* hybrids gave us another impressive Russian red from Exbury – this time 'Karkov'.

Class 45 for subsect. Taliensia trusses produced an outstanding 'Lionel's Triumph'. Who would have thought that this *R. lacteum* cross languished at the back of an Exbury yard, forgotten and overgrown during the war years, and then emerged as something quite special when it first flowered in 1954.

Class 50 for subsect. Triflora hybrid sprays showed a stunning 'St Tudy' crammed with lobelia blue flowers. This lovely E J P Magor hybrid from Exbury ran 'Dora Amateis' very close for the event's best spray.

Class 55 for Vireyas. These fascinating exotics appear to be undergoing something of a revival since, in recent years, we, in rhododendron circles, have read and seen much more of them. I say 'revival' as they were first introduced into the West in the 1800s and by the 1850s, Veitch had bred more than 500 different hybrids. The question is, where are they now? Well, one of them, 'Princess Alexandra', was displayed by Exbury. With its elegantly long and slender corollas it came runner-up to the same garden's 'Coral Flare'. Coral pink of course but teasingly complicated with hints of other hues like vermillion and orange – very Vireya.

The only classes where Exbury exhibits were beaten were the following.

Class 40 for subsect. Campylocarpa hybrid trusses. Brian Wright won this with that charming old Slocock cross, 'Unique' and somewhat ironically came second with the Exbury-bred hybrid 'Carita Golden Dream'.

Class 42 for *R. thomsonii* hybrid trusses. This was also won by Brian Wright showing a nice but unnamed cerise red. It beat Exbury's good, soft pink and scented 'Aurora' into second place.

Class 47 for subsects. Arborea and Argyrophyllum hybrid trusses. In this class Exbury showed an old favourite, 'Boddaertianum'. It was bred from *R. campanulatum* × *R. arboreum* subsp. *cinnamomeum* in 1863 by Van Houtte and is still a most worthy garden plant. In spite of its long-standing merits, however, the judges, on the day, regarded it as not good enough to outdo Brian Wright's stylish 'Sir Charles Lemon' and A W Simons' striking, deep crimson 'Bibani'. And dare we say it, yet another Exbury creation.

Brian Wright

EARLY CAMELLIA COMPETITION

CICELY PERRING

The winter of 1999/2000 brought us warm weather with few frosts, none particularly severe. As a result the camellia display was lavish – even cultivars that had previously failed to do their duty performed magnificently. 2000 showed every sign of being a spectacular camellia year and so it proved to be.

It is interesting to speculate on the difference between the start of the 20th century and the 21st century. Many of our familiar, beautiful and prolific cultivars did not then grace gardens. Few of the varieties which the Victorians had treasured in their greenhouses have survived – 'Adolphe Audusson', 'Chandleri Elegans' and 'Tricolour' being the exceptions – but consider all the new arrivals which have emerged now that it is realised how very cold hardy camellias can be (although not all camellias are equally tough).

The early Camellia Competition held on the 14 and 15 March 2000 was well supported.

Division 1 – sprays

Classes 1 and 2. On the whole these classes were disappointing although Marigold Assinder won second and fourth places in Class 1 and second in Class 2 with 'Lily Pons', 'Desire' and 'Debbie', while Ann

Hooton was third in Class 1 with 'Rubescens Major', third in Class 2 with 'Mary Larcom', and second in Class 3 with 'Lasca Beauty'.

There were seven entries in Class 10 for any three single-flowered cultivars. Ann Hooton took first place with a lively 'Sylvia'.

Class 11 for only one single-flowered cultivar had 17 entries. Again Ann Hooton took first place with 'Sylvia'. Chatsworth House Trust came second and third showing a fine 'Jupiter' – lovely white mottling.

Class 12. There were 11 entries of three semi-double cultivars. First was Mrs Petherick with 'Mrs D. W. Davis', 'Lady in Red' and 'Grandiflora'. Second and third was D R Strauss. Particularly fine of his entry were 'Midnight' and 'White Nun'. Chatsworth House Trust came fourth and another entry was commended. Of this exhibit 'Bob Hope' was exceptional and 'Herme' in the second entry was a very interesting bloom with a white edged petal – a cultivar not often exhibited.

Class 14 for any semi-double cultivar had 23 entries. This class enjoyed a display of blooms of exceptional beauty. First was D R Strauss with 'White Nun', second and fourth Mr Betteley with 'Lady Clare' and 'Drama Girl' while K T Powell was third with 'Ruddigore'. Mrs J G Totty was commended with 'R. L. Wheeler'.

Class 14, any three anemone- or peony-formed cultivars, one bloom of each. The class attracted 12 entries. First place went to Chatsworth House Trust with 'Midnight Elegans' and 'Dixie Knight', second was A W Simons with a sport of 'Elegans Supreme', 'Margaret Davis' and 'Brushfield's Yellow' and third went to Ann Hooton with 'Miss Charleston', 'A. M. Wilson' and 'R. L. Wheeler'. Fourth was Edmund de Rothschild with 'Kramer's Supreme', 'Elegans Champagne' and 'Chandleri Elegans'.

Class 15 for any anemone- or peony-formed cultivars had 23 entries. First place was Chatsworth House Trust with 'Nuccio's Jewel', second and third to Mr Betteley with 'Little Bit' and 'Margaret Davis' (see Fig. 28) which was a very lovely example of a beautiful camellia, as indeed that exhibited by Edmund de Rothschild who was awarded a fourth place.

Class 16, any rose-formed or formal double, one of each. This class attracted 11 entries. First was David Davis with 'Nuccio's Gem', 'Diana's Charm' and 'Matterhorn', second was Chatsworth House Trust with 'Alba Plena', 'Mathotiana Rubra' and 'Nuccio's Pearl' and third was Josephine Newman with 'Sawada's Dream', 'Wilamena' and 'Commander Mulroy'. Ann Hooton's exhibit included a superb 'Twilight'. D R Strauss included 'Fashionata' and Edmund de Rothschild's 'Roger Hall' – all lovely flowers.

Class 17 for any rose-formed or formal double cultivars had 19 entries. First was Ann Hooton with 'Twilight', second

David Davis with 'Nuccio's Gem', third was Mrs Petherick with 'Te Deum' and fourth, David Davis with 'Berenice Perfection'. Chatsworth House Trust was highly commended for their entry of 'Nuccio's Pearl'.

Class 18 required any six cultivars of mixed japonicas, one bloom of each and attracted 11 entries – a wonderful show of 66 blooms. First was Edmund de Rothschild, second Ann Hooton, third A W Simons and fourth Chatsworth House Trust. The entries all included cultivars already exhibited in other entries. Particularly delightful was Ann Hooton's 'Twilight' which has had a most successful run.

Class 19, any three cultivars of mixed japonicas, one bloom of each. There were 15 entries. Ann Hooton came first with 'Royalty', 'Dr Clifford Parks' and 'Lasca Beauty'. Second was David Davis with 'Elegans Champagne' (a really superb bloom), 'Guilio Nuccio' and 'Nuccio's Gem'. Third was Mr Betteley with 'Nuccio's Pearl', 'Yours Truly' and 'Margaret Davis'. Fourth, Chatsworth House with 'Midnight', 'Jean Clere' and 'Elegans' while Edmund de Rothschild was highly commended for his entry of 'Drama Girl', 'Kramer's Supreme' and 'Dear Jenny'.

Class 20, any three hybrids, one bloom of each. There were 14 entries. No first was awarded but second went to Mr Betteley with 'Otto Hopfer', 'Dr Clifford Parks' and 'Valentines Day'. Third was Ann Hooton with 'Anticipation', 'Dr L. Polizzi' and 'Francie L.' and fourth, A W Simons with 'Debut', 'Interval' and 'Otto Hopfer'. Chatsworth House Trust was highly recommended showing 'Dainty

Dale', 'Mary Phoebe Taylor' and 'Francie L.' while Edmund de Rothschild was commended for his entry of 'Anticipation', 'Donation' and 'Carnation'.

Class 21, for any *Camellia reticulata* hybrid of which one parent is *C. × williamsii* or *C. saluenensis*, had 7 entries. First was Ann Hooton with 'Francie L.', second Mrs R Barker with a superb bloom of 'Buddha' and third, Mr Betteley with 'Inspiration'.

Class 22, for any *C. reticulata* species or hybrid, had 15 entries. This was a magnificent display of blooms that must have taxed the judges. First was David Davis with 'Harold L. Paige' (see front cover), second Ann Hooton with 'Dr Clifford Parks' and third Chatsworth House Trust with 'Captain Rawes'.

Class 23, for any three *C. × williamsii*, one bloom of each, attracted eight entries. First was Ann Hooton with 'Elegant Beauty', 'Hope' and 'Anticipation'. Second and third was Chatsworth House Trust with respectively (1) 'Anticipation', 'Debbie' and 'Daintiness' and (2) 'Waterlily', 'El Dorado' and 'Dainty Dale'. Fourth was Edmund de Rothschild with 'Anticipation', 'Donation' and 'Brigadoon'.

Class 24, any single *C. × williamsii*, attracted 13 entries. First was D R Strauss with 'Mary Jobson', second Chatsworth House Trust with 'Muskoka' and third, Brian Wright with 'Mary Christian'.

Class 25, any semi-double *C. × williamsii*. First was Chatsworth House Trust with 'Daintiness', second Ann Hooton with 'Brigadoon', third A W Simons with 'Senorita' and fourth, Marigold Assinder with 'Brigadoon'.

Class 26 for any peony- or anemone-formed *C. × williamsii*, had 17 entries. First was David Davis with 'Senorita', second Chatsworth House Trust with 'Debbie', third Edmund de Rothschild with 'Carnation', while D R Strauss's 'Debbie' was highly commended

Class 27, for any hybrid other than *C. reticulata* or *C. × williamsii*, had six entries. First was David Davis with 'Nicky Crisp', second D R Strauss with 'Barbara Hillier', third D R Strauss with 'Betty Ridley' and fourth Ann Hooton with 'Tristram Carlyon'.

Class 28, any yellow cultivar, attracted nine entries. First was A W Simons with 'Brushfield's Yellow', second Mr Betteley with 'Gwenneth Morey', third D R Strauss with 'Brushfield's Yellow', followed by Josephine Newman in fourth also with 'Brushfield's Yellow'.

Class 29, any species, one bloom, had eight entries. First was A W Simons with *C. transnokoensis* – a wonderful tiny white bloom not previously exhibited by Mr Simons. He also took second and third with *C. cuspidata* and *C. saluenensis* respectively. In total five of the eight were by Mr Simons.

Cicely Perring

MAIN CAMELLIA COMPETITION

CICELY PERRING

The Main Camellia Competition was held on the 11 and 12 April 2000. It was a beautiful display with some superb entries. We are very indebted to those members who give the show such enduring support. There is no doubt that these exhibitions of camellia flowers entice the general public and convert many to becoming growers – perhaps potential exhibitors at some future time.

Division 1 – sprays
This division attracted few entries.

Class 1 was for any three sprays, one of each. There were only two entries. First was awarded to Ann Hooton with 'Miss Charleston', 'Bridal Gown' and 'Betty Sheffield Supreme', a really superb bloom.

Class 2, for any three japonica cultivars, was again won by Ann Hooton with 'Pink Pagodo, 'Angel' (a lovely white which seemed to be unblemished) and 'Elegans', an old but very beautiful cultivar. I shall tell mine what a beautiful specimen I have seen to encourage it.

Class 3 for any *C. japonica* was won by Marigold Assinder with a fine bloom of 'Konronkoku'. Sadly hers was the only entry.

Class 4 for any *C. × williamsii* cultivar. Ann Hooton was back in business with a

first for 'Ladies Maid' and second with 'Jury's Yellow'.

There was then a jump to class 10 which is the Leonardslee Bowl. This class demanded 12 different blooms, one of each. It was an education in camellias with six entries showcasing 72 beautiful blooms from many different cultivars.

First place and the Leonardslee Bowl was awarded to A W Simons for his superb entry showing 'Wildfire', 'Desire' and 'Strawberry Parfait', an unknown reticulata seedling, 'Lily Pons', an 'R.L. Wheeler' variety, 'Mercury', 'Valentines Day', 'Lasca Beauty' and 'Augusto Pinto'.

Second was Edmund de Rothschild with 'Strawberry Parfait', 'R.L. Wheeler', 'Lady Clare', 'Tiffany', 'Pride of Descaso', 'Donckelarii', 'Nagasaki', 'Kumaska', 'Elsie Jury', 'Reg Raglan', 'Drama Girl' and 'Kramer's Supreme'. The bloom of 'Nagasaki' was quite exceptional.

Third came D R Strauss showing 'Tom Thumb', 'Berenice Boddy', an unknown, 'Black Lace', 'C. M. Hovey', 'Konronkoku', 'Virgins Blush', 'Fimbriata', 'Otome', 'Katherine Nuccio', 'Dona Herzilia de Freitas Magalhaes' and 'Waltzing Time'. D R Strauss had another entry which, while unplaced, was interesting in that he brought together five cultivars with deckle-edged petals and very pretty names – 'Pink Cinderella', 'Fred Saunders', 'Clarke Hubbs', 'Elegans Splendor' and 'Hawaii'. Fourth came Ann Hooton with 'Francie L.', 'Elegans Splendor', 'Grand Prix', 'Henry Turnbull', 'Leo Jury', 'Elegans Supreme', 'R.L. Wheeler', 'Mona Jury', 'Angel Royalty', 'Satan's Robe' and 'Dr Clifford Parks'.

Class 11 was not quite so demanding as class 10 but still required six cultivars, one bloom of each. First was David Davis with 'Nuccio's Pearl', 'Nuccio's Gem', 'William Bartlett', 'Diana's Charm' (see Fig. 30), 'Shire Chan' and 'Kramer's Supreme'. Second was Edmund de Rothschild with 'Swann', 'Ballet Queen', 'Nuccio's Jewel', 'Adolphe Audusson', 'Grandiflora Alba' and 'Yesterday'. Third was D R Strauss with 'Angel', 'Tomorrow', ' Park Hill', 'Betty Sheffield Supreme', 'Silver Ruffles', 'Drama Girl' and 'Apollo'. D R Strauss also took fourth place with 'Hakurakuten', 'Mikenjaku' (a name now considered to be a synonym for 'Nagasaki', first brought to the Channel Islands in 1887), 'C.M. Wilson', 'Duchesse Decazes Pink', 'Marie Bracey' and an 'Adolphe Audusson' variety.

Class 12. There were five entries in this class for single cultivars of *C. japonica,* one bloom of three cultivars. First was A W Simons with 'Ohkan', 'Adelina Patty' and 'Red Cardinal' (see Fig. 22), second Edmund de Rothschild with 'Jupiter', 'Furo-an' and 'Rogetsu', and third was Ann Hooton with 'Henry Turnbull', 'Juno' and 'Jennifer Turnbull'.

Class 13, for any single-flowered *C. japonica,* had six entries. First was Ann Hooton with 'Henry Turnbull', second Ann Hooton with 'Furo-an' and third, Edmund de Rothschild with 'Hatsuzakara'.

Class 14 was for any three semi-double cultivars, one bloom of each. There were six entries. First was Edmund de Rothschild with 'Lady Clare', 'Drama Girl' and 'R.L. Wheeler'. Second was D R Strauss with 'Adolphe Audusson', 'Hakurakuten' (also known as 'Refugee' and 'Wisley White') and 'Mrs D.W. Davis' and third, Ann Hooton with 'Angel', 'Grand Prix' and 'Hakurakuten'.

Class 15 for any semi-double *C. japonica* cultivar had nine entries. First was A W Simons with 'Wildfire', second Ann Hooton with 'Angel' and third, Edmund de Rothschild with 'R.L. Wheeler'.

Class 16, any three anemone- and peony-formed cultivars of *C. japonica*, one bloom of each, had seven entries. First was David Davis showing 'Kramer's Supreme', 'Swan Lake' and 'Tiffany', second Ann Hooton showing 'Elegans Supreme', 'Miss Charleston' and 'R.L. Wheeler' and third, D R Strauss with 'Reg Ragland', 'Blood of China' and 'Elegans Supreme'. Edmund de Rothschild was highly commended for 'Nuccio's Jewel' (see Fig. 29), 'Tom Knudsen' and 'Daikagura'.

Class 17 for any anemone- or peony-formed cultivar had eight entries. First was David Davis with a beautiful bloom of 'Elegans', second Ann Hooton with 'R.L. Wheeler', third D R Strauss with 'Elegans Splendor' and fourth, A W Simons with 'R.L. Wheeler'.

Class 18, any three rose-formed or formal double cultivars, one bloom of each, had eight entries. First was Ann Hooton who showed 'Twilight', 'Annie Wylam' and 'Leo Jury'. 'Twilight' was an exceptionally lovely bloom. Second was David Davis who showed 'Nuccio's Pearl', 'C.M. Hovey' and 'Nuccio's Gem'. David Davis also took third with 'Twilight', 'Nuccio's Gem' and 'Diana's Charm'. In fourth was Edmund de Rothschild with 'C.M. Hovey', 'Madame de Bois' and 'Hanatachibana' while D R Strauss received a highly commended for 'Otome', 'Katherine Nuccio' and 'Tom Thumb'.

Class 19 for any rose-formed or formal double cultivar had 10 entries. First was 'Nuccio's Pearl' exhibited by David Davis', second 'Elizabeth Anderson' by Mrs J G Totty, third D R Strauss showing 'Lavinia Maggi' and fourth A W Simons showing 'Augusto Pinto'.

Class 20 for any three cultivars other than cultivars of *C. japonica*, had eight entries. First was David Davis showing 'Nicky Crisp', 'Senorita' and 'Harold L. Paige'. Second was Ann Hooton with 'Bridal Gown', 'Wilbur Foss' and 'Mona Jury'. Third was Ann Hooton again with 'Francie L.', 'Royalty' and 'Dr Clifford Parks'. Fourth was D R Strauss showing 'Waltzing Time', 'Black Lace' and a nice red. A W Simons was highly commended for 'Black Opal', 'Lasca Beauty' and 'Innovation'.

Class 21 for any *C. reticulata* species or hybrid had nine entries. The top three prizes went to A W Simons, first for 'Lasca Beauty', second 'Dr Clifford Parks' and third 'Valentines Day'. Edmund de Rothschild was highly commended for 'Pagoda'.

Class 22, any three *C. × williamsii*

cultivars, one bloom of each. There were five entries. First was Ann Hooton showing 'Elegant Beauty', 'Bridal Gown' and 'Mona Jury'. Second A W Simons showing 'Anticipation', 'Debbie' and 'Ballet Queen'. Third was Edmund de Rothschild showing 'E.G. Waterhouse', 'Debbie' and 'Anticipation'. Fouth was D R Strauss showing 'Waltzing Time', 'Mirage' and 'E.G. Waterhouse'.

Class 23, any single-flowered *C. × williamsii*, one bloom. There were seven entries. First was Ann Hooton with 'St Ewe', second A W Simons showing the scented red 'Trewithen' and third A W Simons again with 'St Ewe'.

Class 24 for any semi-double *C. × williamsii* cultivar, one bloom, had eight entries. First was Ann Hooton with 'Lady's Maid', second A W Simons with 'Waltzing Time' and third Mrs J C Totty with 'Mirage'. Ann Hooton also received a highly commended with 'Brigadoon'.

Class 25 for any anemone- or peony-formed *C. × williamsii* cultivar, one bloom, had 10 entries. First was Ann Hooton with a variety of 'Ballet Queen', second Mrs J C Totty with 'Anticipation' and third, D R Strauss with 'Jury's Yellow'. A W Simons was highly commended with 'Elsie Jury'.

Class 26, any rose-formed or formal double *C. × williamsii* cultivar, one bloom. There were six entries. D R Strauss was first and second with 'Julia Hamiter' and 'E.G. Waterhouse'. Ann Hooton took third with 'Rose Parade' and A W Simons fourth with 'Gwavas'.

Class 27 for any species or hybrid not specified above, one bloom, had seven entries. First was David Davis showing

'Nicky Crisp', second A W Simons with 'Honey Moon' – a lovely creamy flower with a strong yellow tendency towards the centre if grown under glass. It was produced from 'Guilio Nuccio Pitardii' × 'Chrysantha', a good portent for some beautiful new blooms in the future. Third was A W Simons showing 'Sowgas Parlova' and fourth D R Strauss with *C. saluenensis*.

Class 28, for any arrangement of camellias shown for effect (75cm x 75cm [2¹/₂ × 2¹/₂ft]) using no other plant material, had three entries. Mrs E Bullivant took first with a sensitive use and beautiful arrangement of various camellia flowers. In second place Ann Hooton displayed blooms of 'Lady Lock' while in third Edmund de Rothchild's lovely blooms may have benefited from a better display. This was an altogether beautiful class which should quickly attract more entries.

Cicely Perring

AWARDS

Award of Merit
Camellia japonica '**Canon Boscawen**'.
AM 14 March 2000 as a hardy flowering plant for exhibition. Flowers informal peony form, no stamens visible, 80mm diameter, white; outer petals 45 × 40mm; inner petals irregular. Leaves broadly obovate, shining mid green. Origin obscure, originating from Tregothnan. Exhibited by Hon Evelyn Boscawen, Tregothnan, Truro, Cornwall TR2 4AN. Standard Specimen and transparency in Herb. Hort. Wisley (WSY).

Camellia japonica '**In the Pink**' (Parentage unrecorded). AM 14 March 2000 as a hardy flowering plant for exhibition. Flowers formal double (slight wavy edge to petals gives it some depth), 100mm diameter, pink (52C) throughout, c.57 petals; outer petals 45 × 45mm; inner petals 25 × 25mm. Leaves broadly elliptic, shining dark green. Raised by Kramer Bros, USA. Exhibited by Dr J A Smart, Marwood Hill, Barnstaple, Devon EX31 4EB. Specimen and transparency in Herb. Hort. Wisley (WSY).

Camellia japonica '**Spring Sonnet**' (Sport of 'Colonial Lady'). AM 14 March 2000 as a hardy flowering plant for exhibition. Flowers open informal semi-double to peony form with small cluster of stamens visible in centre, 110mm diameter. Petals pale pink (62D) with irregular,

c.7mm wide edge of deeper pink (62A) and occasional streaks of deeper pink descending to base of petal; outer petals 45 × 40mm; inner petals irregular and wavy. Leaves elliptic, moderately shiny, dark green. Raised by V. O McCaskill, USA. Exhibited by Dr J A Smart, Marwood Hill, Barnstaple, Devon EX31 4EB. Specimen and transparency in Herb. Hort. Wisley (WSY).

Rhododendron '**Birthday Girl**' (*R. yakushimanum* hybrid). AM 22 May 2000 as a hardy flowering plant for exhibition. Rounded truss of c.16 flowers, 130mm in diameter. Corolla 40 × 40mm, campanulate; tube 20mm; lobes 20 × 22mm, overlapping, with wavy edges. Bud pink (63B). Inside of corolla and lobes very pale pink (69A) with 2 narrow flares (20 × 3mm) of dark pink spotting extending from corolla tube base to sinus either side of upper lobe; outside of corolla tube pink (68A). Stamens 7-10, 15-20mm, included in tube; filaments pink with white pubescence at base; anthers pale brown. Style 30mm, pink (58B); stigma pale brown with pink spots; ovary white pubescent. Calyx insignificant, to 2mm. Pedicel 15-30mm, pink with scattered pubescence. Leaves evergreen, narrowly elliptic, 90 × 30mm, underside with very thin, pale brown, plastered indumentum. Crossed, raised and exhibited by Mr Edmund de Rothschild, Exbury Gardens, Exbury, Southampton,

Hampshire SO45 1AZ. Standard Specimen in Specimen in Herb. Hort. Wisley (WSY).

***Rhododendron* 'Golden Clipper'** ('Crest' [male] × 'New Comet' [female]). AM 27 April 1999, as a hardy flowering plant for exhibition. Rounded truss of c. 12 flowers. Flowers fragrant. Flower bud greyish-red (182B). Corolla widely funnel-shaped, 40 ˇ 70 mm, 7-lobed, greenish-yellow (4A-B) inside and out with no internal or external markings. Stamens 14; filaments pale yellow; anthers pale brown. Style pale yellowish-green, glandular at base; ovary green, glandular. Calyx rudimentary with irregular lobes to 2 mm. Pedicel 20 mm, slightly glandular. Leaves oblong, glabrous, to 110 ˇ 55 mm, apex rounded, base cordate to rounded, upper surface mid green, lower surface slightly glaucous. Petiole 25 mm, heavily flushed maroon. Specimen and transparency in Herb. Hort. Wisley (WSY). Crossed and raised by A F George. Exhibited by Hydon Nurseries, Clock Barn Lane, Hydon Heath, Godalming, Surrey GU8 4AZ.

***Rhododendron* 'Hydon Amethyst'** ('Blue Diamond' × *R. russatum*). AM 25 April 2000 as a hardy flowering plant for exhibition. Loose truss of c.5 flowers. Corolla widely funnel-shaped, 15 × 40mm, purple (82A ageing to 83B), paler at base of tube externally, unspotted; tube 5mm, dense pubescence at mouth; upper lobes oblong, 14 × 10mm; lower lobes oblong, 16 × 10mm. Stamens 10, 20-30mm, exserted; filaments purple (82B), densely white pubescent at base. Style 30mm, red-purple

(71B), white pubescent at base; ovary green, scaly, pubescent. Calyx rudimentary with irregular lobes to 4mm. Pedicel to 15mm, heavily red-flushed, scaly. Leaves evergreen, elliptic, to 55 × 20mm; upper surface dark green with reticulate venation; lower surface paler with sparse mixture of pale brown and dark brown scales. Crossed and raised by A F George. Exhibited by Hydon Nurseries, Clock Barn Lane, Hydon Heath, Godalming, Surrey GU8 4AZ. Standard Specimen and transparency in Herb. Hort. Wisley (WSY).

***Rhododendron* 'Hydon Rodney'** (Azamia Group × *R. augustinii*). AM 25 April 2000 as a hardy flowering plant for exhibition. Compact truss of c.11 flowers. Corolla widely funnel-shaped opening flat, 12 × 55mm, 5-6 lobed, violet-blue (92A ageing to 93B) but distinctly paler in centre and at base of tube externally, 2 rays of green to brown spotting extending for 15mm from centre of corolla to sinus either side of upper lobe, scattered scales externally; tube 5mm, slight pubescence at mouth; upper lobes broadly ovate, 17 × 15mm; lower lobes ovate, 22 × 17mm. Stamens 10, 35-40mm, exserted and curved upwards; filaments violet (84A), densely white pubescent at base; anthers pale brown. Style 35-40mm, purple (77C), glabrous; stigma brown; ovary green with green scales and scattered hairs. Calyx rudimentary with occasional narrow lobe to 5mm, green. Pedicel to 15mm, green with red flush. Leaves evergreen, elliptic, to 40 × 16mm; upper surface dark green with reticulate venation; lower surface paler with sparse, pale brown, rimmed scales. Crossed and

, 22 *(below left):* Camellia *'Red Cardinal',* winner of Class
for Andrew Simons at the Main Camellia Competition
)0 *(see p.76)*
, 23 *(right):* Magnolia *'Heaven Scent'* in Sunderland
race, London W2 (see p.55)
, 24 *(bottom):* Magnolia campbellii *'Betty Jessel'.* An entry
the photographic competition from J P Chatelard,
tographed in his garden near Baie du Mont-Saint-Michel

Fig 25 (left): Rhododendron campanulatum, *the winner of Class for Exbury Gardens at the Main Rhododendron Competition (see p.68*
Fig. 26 (below): Rhododendron fulvum, *another winner for Exbury Class 2 (spray of any species) at the E Rhododendron Competition (see p.6(*

. 27: Rhododendron pachysanthum, *winner of ss 3 and the McLaren Cup for Dr R Jack (see p.68)*

Fig. 28: Camellia *'Margaret Davies', fourth in Class 15 at the Early Camellia Competition (see p.73)*

. 29: Camellia *'Nuccio's Jewel', an entry from ∙mund de Rothschild at the Main Camellia ∙mpetition (see p.76)*

Fig. 30: Camellia *'Diana's Charm'. Winner of Class 11 for David Davis at the Main Camellia Competition (see p.76)*

Fig. 31 (above): Rhododendron *'Cinnkeys'* (R. cinnabarinum *subsp.* cinnabarinum × R. keysii).
Winner of the Photographic Competition for Mr J L Rees.
Fig. 32 (below left): Magnolia *'Mark Jury'*
(M. mollicomata *'Lanarth'* × M. sargentiana robusta),
second in the Photographic Competition, taken by Dr George Hargreaves at Trehane Garden, Cornwall.
Fig. 33 (right): Third in the Photographic Competition. An azalea seedling related to R. *'Altaclarensis' and grown in his Anglesey garden by John Wilkes-Jones (see p.54)*

raised by A F George. Exhibited by Hydon Nurseries, Clock Barn Lane, Hydon Heath, Godalming, Surrey GU8 4AZ. Standard Specimen and transparency in Herb. Hort. Wisley (WSY).

***Rhododendron* 'Tower Dexter'** (*R. atlanticum* × unknown). AM 22 May 2000 as a hardy flowering plant for exhibition. A deciduous azalea (Cote hybrid). Loose truss of c.12 flowers, 120cm in diameter. Bud orange-pink (42D). Corolla funnel-shaped, 45 × 50mm, 5 lobed; tube 20 × 4mm, red (45D) with white glandular hairs to 1mm; lower 4 lobes 25 × 14mm, white heavily suffused pink (62B-C) especially on midrib and reverse; upper lobe 25 × 18mm, same colour as other lobes but also with speckled blotch of yellow (17B). Stamens 5, 60mm, exserted; filaments white with some pink and yellow flushing, white pubescent at base only; anthers pale brown. Style 60mm, pink flushed, pubescent at base; stigma green; ovary with long, dense, white hairs. Calyx with 5 irregular green lobes to 4mm, pubescent. Pedicel 10-15mm, green with red flush,

pubescent. Leaves (at anthesis) obovate, to 55 × 22mm; margin with ciliate hairs which are also scattered on upper surface and midrib beneath. Raised by J B Stevenson. Exhibited by Hydon Nurseries, Clock Barn Lane, Hydon Heath, Godalming, Surrey GU8 4AZ. Standard Specimen in Herb. Hort. Wisley (WSY).

First Class Certificate
***Camellia* 'Tom Knudsen'** (*C. japonica* × *C. reticulata*). FCC 11 April 2000 as a hardy flowering plant for exhibition. Flowers rose-form double with scattered stamens in centre, 90mm diameter, dark red (46A). Leaves broadly elliptic, dark green. Raised by F. Maitland, USA. Exhibited by Dr J A Smart, Marwood Hill, Barnstaple, Devon EX31 4EB. Specimen and transparency in Herb. Hort. Wisley (WSY).

Erratum 1999
Under *Rhododendron veitchianum* Cubittii Group 'Penelope Jack', for 'hardy flowering plant for exhibition' read 'flowering plant for exhibition'.

RHS Rhododendron and Camellia Committee

Chairman
J G Hillier, c/o Hillier Nurseries, Ampfield House, Ampfield, Romsey, Hants SO51 9PA

Vice-Chairman
J T Gallagher, Oldfield, 29 Moorlands Road, Verwood, Dorset BH31 6PD

Members
Lady Aberconway, Bodnant, Tal-y-Cafn, Colwyn Bay, Clwyd LL28 5RE
Lord Aberconway, VMH, Bodnant, Tal-y-Cafn, Colwyn Bay, Clwyd LL28 5RE
B Archibold, Starveacre, Dalwood, Axminster, East Devon EX13 7HH
J D Bond, LVO, VMH, Georgia Lodge, Buckhurst Road, Cheapside, Ascot, Berks SL5 7RP
The Hon. Edward Boscawen, Garden House, High Beeches Lane, Handcross, Sussex
    RH17 6HQ
M Flanagan, Verderers, Wick Road, Englefield Green, Egham, Surrey TW20 3AE
M Foster, White House Farm, Ivy Hatch, Sevenoaks, Kent TN15 0NN
A F George, Hydon Nurseries, Hydon Heath, Godalming, Surrey GU9 4AZ
Dr R Jack, Edgemoor, Loch Road, Lanark ML11 9BG
D G Millais, Crosswater Farm, Churt, Farnham, Surrey GU10 2JN
M Pharoah, Marwood Hill, Marwood, Barnstaple, Devon EX31 4EB
A Simons, Wingfield House, 11 Brinsmade Road, Ampthill, Bedfordshire
A V Skinner, MBE, 2 Frog Firle Cottage, Alfriston, nr Polegate, E Sussex BN26 5TT
M O Slocock, VMH, Knap Hill Nursery, Barrs Lane, Knaphill, Woking, Surrey GU21 2JW
Major T le M Spring-Smyth, 1 Elcombe's Close, Lyndhurst, Hants SO43 7DS
O R Staples, 6 Chestnut Way, Adel, Leeds, W Yorks LS16 7TN
C Tomlin, Starborough Nursery, Starborough Road, Marsh Green, Edenbridge, Kent
    TN8 5RB
Miss J Trehane, Church Cottage, Hampreston, Wimborne, Dorset BH21 7LX
C H Williams, Burncoose Nurseries, Gwennap, Redruth, Cornwall TR16 6BJ
F J Williams, Caerhays Castle, Gorran, St Austell, Cornwall PL26 6LY
M Grant, RHS Garden Wisley (Secretary)

RHS Rhododendron, Camellia and Magnolia Group

— ❧ —

Officers

Chairman Mr Maurice C FOSTER, White House Farm, Ivy Hatch, Sevenoaks, Kent
TN15 0NN (Tel: 01732 810634)

Hon. Treasurer Mr Chris WALKER, 81 Station Road, Shepley, Huddersfield, W Yorks
HD8 8DS (Tel: 01484 604922, Fax: 01484 602973)

Hon. Secretary Mrs Josephine M WARREN, Netherton, Buckland Monachorum, Yelverton,
Devon PL20 7NL (Tel/fax: 01822 854022)

Hon. Membership Secretary Mr Tony WESTON, Whitehills, Newton Stewart, Scotland
DG8 6SL (Tel: 01671 402049, Fax: 01671 403106, email:
tony@rhodo.demon.co.uk)

Hon. Tours Organizer Mrs Valerie ARCHIBOLD, Starveacre, Dalwood, Axminster, Devon
EX13 7HH (Tel: 01404 881221)

Hon. Year Book Editor Mr Philip D EVANS, West Netherton, Drewsteignton, Devon
EX6 6RB (Tel: 01647 281285, email: philip.d.evans@talk21.com)

Hon. Bulletin Editor Mrs Eileen WHEELER, Llwyngoras, Velindre, Crymych, Dyfed
SA41 3XW (Tel: 01239 820464, email: e.wheeler@btinternet.com)

Committee Members

Mr David N FARNES, 5 Pine View (off Deerlands Road), Ashgate, Chesterfield, Derbyshire
S40 4DN (Tel: 01246 272105)

Mr Martin D C GATES, 12 Marlborough Road, Chandlers Ford, Eastleigh, Hants SO53
5DH (Tel: 01703 252843)

Mr John D HARSANT, Newton House, Wall Lane, Heswell, Wirral, Merseyside L60 8NF
(Tel: 0151 342 3664)

Dr R H L JACK, Edgemoor, Loch Road, Lanark ML11 9BG (Tel: 01555 663021)

Miss Cicely E PERRING, Watermill House, Watermill Lane, Pett, E Sussex TN35 4HY (Tel:
01424 812103)

Mr Alastair STEVENSON, 24 Bolton Road, Grove Park, London W4 3TB (Tel: 0181 742
7571, Fax: 0181 987 8728, email: stevensonmpa@compuserve.com

Mr Ivor T STOKES, Pantcoch, Carmel, Llanelli, Dyfed SA14 7SG (Tel: 01269 844048)

Branch Chairmen

International Mr Michael JURGENS, The Old House, Silchester, Reading, Berkshire
RG7 2LU (Tel: 01189 700240, Fax: 01189 701682)

N Ireland Mr Patrick FORDE, Seaforde, Downpatrick, Co Down BT30 8PG
(Tel: 01396 811225, Fax: 01396 811370)

New Forest Mr Christopher FAIRWEATHER, The Garden Centre, High Street, Beaulieu,
Hants SO42 7YR (Tel: 01590 612307, Fax: 01590 612519)

Norfolk Mrs J M IDIENS, Beaconswood, Roman Camp, Sandy Lane, West Runton,
Cromer, Norfolk NR27 9ND (Tel: 01263 837779)

North Wales and Northwest Mr J Ken HULME, Treshnish, 72 Parkgate Road, Neston,
S Wirral L64 6QQ (Tel: 0151 336 8852)

Peak District Mr David N FARNES, 5 Pine View (off Deerlands Road), Ashgate,
Chesterfield, Derbyshire, S40 4DN (Tel: 01246 272105)

Southeast Mr John E HILLIARD, 99 Gales Drive, Three Bridges, Crawley, Sussex
RH10 1QD (Tel: 01293 522859)

Southwest Dr Alun J B EDWARDS, 12 Ellerslie Road, Barnstaple, Devon, EX31 2HT
(Tel: 01271 343324)

Wessex Mrs Miranda GUNN, Ramster, Petworth Road, Chiddingfold, Surrey GU8 4SN
(Tel: 01428 644422)

Website address

http://www.rhs.org.uk/about/mn_contact_rhododendron.asp

INDEX

Glendoick Gardens Ltd
Glendoick
Perth PH2 7NS
Scotland
TEL 01738 860205
E MAIL sales@glendoick.com
web site: www.glendoick.com

GHLIGHTS OF OUR NEW 70-PAGE, FULLY
SCRIPTIVE COLOUR CATALOGUE,
ODODENDRONS, AZALEAS, CAMELLIAS,
MULAS, MECONOPSIS AND OTHER PLANTS.
ND £2.

IL ORDER, EXPORT OR COLLECT FROM
R NURSERY. PLANTS CAN BE SENT
TOBER-1ST APRIL. OUTSIDE THIS PERIOD,
AILABLE FROM GLENDOICK GARDEN
NTRE ONLY.

PHALANTHUM NMAIENSE GROUP. ☛ C.V.
3 from S.E. Tibet. Usually with pale yellow flowers
ugh some forms are cream or pale pink. Seems to be a
d doer. First time introduced by Kenneth Cox.

ENDOICK ®™ RUBY ☛ ☛ ('Lampion' x
armaine') 50cm (18") H4-5? A new Glendoick hybrid
very fine waxy deep red flowers with a large calyx
no stamens. Very slow-growing with deep green
es and attractive reddish buds all winter. Ideal to grow
the bird hybrids. Late April-May. ('Glendoick' is a
stered trademark. Variety may not be commercially
luced or sold without permission) (photo p. **)

CH EARN ☛ ☛ ('Hotei' x 'Cupcake' clone A) 1m
H4. A new hybrid of our own, this is the first good
dwarf yellow 'yak' hybrid we have seen. Masses of
yellow flowers on a slow-growing and compact plant.
ds good drainage. Very promising. May.

NUM (Taliensia S.S.) ☛ ☛ 30cm (1ft) spreading.
At last we have a supply of this rare species to satisfy
and. Long a collector's favourite, this slow-growing
ies has glaucous recurved leaves with fawn
mentum. Very compact habit. Flowers (rarely)
my-white in April-May. We offer the R.B. Cooke
e with bluest leaves, the Towercourt clone with
ner leaves and seedlings raised by crossing the above
es.

KERBIRD ☛ ☛ ® (ciliatum x edgeworthii) 1.20m
H3-4. This is a real breakthrough: a compact,
ted dwarf which we can grow outdoors at Glendoick.
es of scented white flowers. Best in a sheltered site.
risingly bud hardy. Early May. Also worth growing
pot plant indoors. The same cross as 'Lady Alice
villiam' but hardier and more compact.

EATEAR ☛ ☛ (keiskei Yaku Fairy x
liferum)1m (3ft) One of the latest of the 'bird' series.

Most unusual tubular cream flowers, striped pink on a
vigorous but tidy grower with bronzy new growth. April.
Not for gardens colder than Glendoick. See also the sister
seedling 'Waxbill'.

BALANGENSE (Grandia S.S.) ☛ ☛ 5m (16ft.)? H4-5
Fine new introduction with handsome foliage with pale
indumentum and white flushed pink flowers. From the
Wolong panda reserve. Rare. April? Grafts.

DENUDATUM C. 7012 (Argyrophylla S.S.) ☛ to 3m
(10ft) H4? Attractive shiny rough leaves with grey-brown
indumentum. Flowers usually rose, spotted or blotched.
Related to *R. floribundum*. A fine new introduction from
C. Sichuan with excellent foliage. April-May?

GLANDULIFERUM C.& H. 7131 (Fortunea S.S.) ☛ ®
☛ 2m (6ft)+ H4? Outstanding recently introduced species
from N.E. Yunnan, with fine, very large leaves, a startling
red when young, glaucous below. 5-7 large, scented
flowers. Vigorous and should prove a winner. May-June.

LANATOIDES (Lanata S.S) ☛ ☛☛ 3-5m (10-16ft) H4-
5. We finally located a population of this elusive species
in 1996 and introduced seed from S.E. Tibet. White
flowers in February-March on a magnificent foliage plant
with thick fawn indumentum on the upper surface and a
light brown covering on the new growth. Mature leaves
dark green. One of the rarest and most desirable species.
Demand certain to outstrip supply.

OCHRACEUM C.& H. 7052 (Maculifera S.S.) ☛ ☛
2.5m (8ft) H4-5? This is perhaps the most important,
distinct and exciting new introduction in recent years.
Rather small, narrow leaves with light brown
indumentum. Striking rich to dark red flowers on an
upright, tidy-growing plant. May?

SINOFALCONERI C.& H. 7183 ☛ ☛ (Falconera S.S.)
5m (16ft)? H3? First offering of this newly introduced
species with foliage rivalling *R. falconeri*. Chinese
photographs show beautiful yellow flowers as fine as
those of *R. macabeanum*. It has come through recent
winters at Glendoick without any damage, so must be
relatively hardy. Very promising. April?

MARLEY HEDGES ☛ ('Anna' x 'Purple Splendour')??
1.2-1.5m (4-5ft). Large, packed trusses of white flowers,
edged strong reddish-purple with a reddish-purple blotch.
Very unusual new American hybrid. Very free-flowering.

PRETTY WOMAN ☛ ('Orange Marmalade' x 'Pink
Petticoats') 2m? (6ft) H4. Enormous multiple-flowered
trusses of frilled pink flowers. Good reports from its
native USA.

RACOON ☛ (Glendoick evergreen azalea) NEW. 30cm
(12"). The latest of our azalea hybrids to flower. Masses
of long-lasting bright red flowers in June-July, on a
compact, spreading plant. Shows great promise.

Rhododendrons & Azaleas

FOR THE CONNOISSEUR FROM **LODER PLANTS**

MAIL ORDER, PLANT CENTRE & EXPORT. TEL:**01403-891412** FAX **891336**.
SEND 2 X1ST STAMPS FOR AVAILABILITY LIST OR VIST OUR WEBSITE AT **www.rhododendrons.com**
OPEN BY APPOINTMENT ONLY. THIS IS SO WE CAN GIVE YOU OUR UNDIVIDED ATTENTION & ADVICE
**(OVER 1000 HYBRIDS, SPECIES AND AZALEAS, EVERGREEN OR DECIDUOUS, EARLY OR LATE
FLOWERING, SCENTED) & ACERS, CAMELLIA'S, MAGNOLIAS AND MANY OTHER CHOICE PLANTS**

JUST SOUTH OF

Leonardslee Gardens

We're sure you'll enjoy a day at Leonardslee so much you'll invest in a season ticket and return again and again! The many miles of walks provide never ending delights and a changing landscape throughout the seasons. There are plenty of quiet spots where you can sit and enjoy one of England's greenest and most pleasant landscapes. The walks extend round the peaceful lakes and waterfalls where wildlife thrives.

Escape from the busy world in Leonardslee's tranquil 240 acres and enjoying the high variety of natural habitats. Watch the large carp in the Waterfall lake and glimpse wallabies and deer in their idyllic setting. Don't miss the Alpine House and Bonsai Exhibition, with lunch or tea in the Clock Tower Restaurant, and before you leave, browse around the good selection of plants for sale at the nursery.

Enjoy the Autumnal glory of Leonardslee where Maples and deciduous Azaleas take on their dramatic shades against the golds and russets of fine woodland trees. Liquidambars, Hickories and Tupelos provide shades of copper and gold. From mid-September until late October the colours change every week. The end of the season can be as dramatic as the beginning

LOWER BEEDING, HORSHAM, W.SUSSEX RH13 6PP. TEL: 01403 891212 FAX: 891305

MILLAIS NURSERIES
RHODODENDRONS

SPECIALIST GROWERS OF
RHODODENDRONS AND AZALEAS

We grow one of the finest ranges of rhododendrons and azaleas in the country, all quality plants at a reasonable price.
Please send 4 x 1st class stamps for our descriptive catalogue.
Our range of 800 different varieties include:

- Choice 'new' species from the Himalayas.
- A selection of the best new hybrids from around the world, and many old favourites, all labelled in our trails ground.
- Specialist late flowering varieties to avoid the frost.
- Big leaved species for the sheltered garden.
- Scented deciduous azaleas for the fragrant garden.
- The versatile evergreen azalea.
- *Yakushimanum* hybrids for the smaller garden.
- Dwarf rhododendrons for the rock garden.
- *Maddenia* series rhododendrons for the conservatory.

We dispatch worldwide
OPEN: Monday - Friday 10am - 1pm, 2 - 5pm
Also: Saturdays in spring and autumn. Daily in May.
Six-acre woodland display garden open in May.

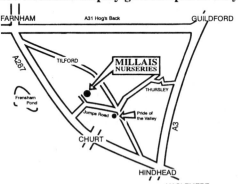

Crosswater Farm, Crosswater Lane, Churt, Farnham, Surrey, GU10 2JN
Tel: (01252) 792698 Fax: (01252) 792526
www.rhododendrons.co.uk